OUTSIDE THE LINES

To Lilia Stella, Adele and Carla Sabrina

Thanks to James 'Jim' Sunderland for sharing my
interests, and for being a great help with the English. To
Carla Sabrina Marenco, that great driving force! To Guia
Camerino for reading and proofreading. To George DuBose
for his enormous enthusiasm and energy. To Sebastiano
Girardi for his brilliant insights. To Alberto Lot for his wise
and indispensable advice. To Mario Panciera of the Venice
Punk Museum for being so readily available. And finally
to Catia Zucchetti, Marina Itolli, Matteo Rosso and Elena
Antonutti for their amazing patience and professionalism.

Lost photographs
of punk and
New Wave's most
iconic albums

Matteo Torcinovich

with
Sebastiano Girardi

OUTSIDE THE LINES

MITCHELL BEAZLEY

Bob Gruen
Various Artists
Max's Kansas City

Roberta Bayley
The Ramones

1976

**New Wave and
the first**

Roberta Bayley
Heartbreakers
L.A.M.F.

1977

Peter "Kodick" Gravelle
The Damned
Damned Damned Damned

Chris Gabrin
Ian Dury
New Boots and Panties!!

Martyn Goddard
The Jam
In the City

Gered Mankowitz
Ultravox!

Masayoshi Sukita
David Bowie
Heroes

Edo Bertoglio
Blondie
Parallel Lines

Martyn Goddard
Blondie
Parallel Lines picture disc

Esther Friedman
Iggy Pop
TV Eye: Live 1977

1978

Chris Gabrin
Elvis Costello
This Year's Model

Keith Collie
Lene Lovich
Stateless

Brian Griffin
Lene Lovich
Stateless

Gered Mankowitz
Generation X

Jim Rakete
Nina Hagen Band

William Christie
Cherry Vanilla
Venus D'Vinyl

George DuBose
The B-52's

Seth Tillett
Lizzy Mercier Descloux
Press Color

1979

Gered Mankowitz
The Tourists
Reality Effect

Martyn Goddard
The Cure
Three Imaginary Boys

Masayoshi Sukita
Yellow Magic Orchestra
Solid State Survivor

Masayoshi Sukita
Sheena & The Rokkets
真空パック (Vacuum Pack)

Brian Griffin
Lene Lovich
Flex

Julia Gorton
Teenage Jesus And the Jerks
Pre Teenage Jesus And The Jerks

Julia Gorton
Teenage Jesus And The Jerks

George DuBose
Lydia Lunch
Queen of Siam

Brian Griffin
Iggy Pop
Soldier

Curtis Knapp
Alan Vega

Rod Swenson
Plasmatics
New Hope for the Wretched

Edo Bertoglio
Plastics
Welcome Back

Ebet Roberts
Suicide
Half Alive

Esther Friedman
Iggy Pop
Zombie Birdhouse

1980   1981   1982

Tony McGee
Public Image Ltd
Second Edition

Alain Bizos
Nina Hagen Band
Unbehagen

Chalkie Davies
The Specials
Specials

Brian Griffin
Joe Jackson
Look Sharp!

Brian Duffy
David Bowie
Lodger

Chalkie Davies
Pretenders

Brian Griffin
Echo and the Bunnymen
Crocodiles

Chris Gabrin
John Foxx
Metamatic

Brian Griffin
Ultravox
Vienna

Andy Earl
Bow Wow Wow
*See Jungle! See Jungle!
Go Join Your Gang Yeah,
City All Over! Go Ape Crazy!*

Fin Costello
Japan
Tin Drum

Brian Griffin
Depeche Mode
A Broken Frame

Eugene Merinov
Bauhaus
*Press the Eject
and Give Me the Tape*

Author **Matteo Torcinovich**

Title **Outside the Lines:**
Lost photographs of punk and
New Wave's most iconic albums

We've all bought an album purely because of its cover, without knowing anything about the music. The look of an album always says something, even if it's just plain white; a white square will always bring to mind the masterpiece of the Beatles' 'White Album', or that wonderful burst of crazy, unlistenable rock from the Italian band Skiantos.

In the vinyl era – unlike after the arrival of CDs – LP covers weren't merely images that represented the musical product. They were created with it, and remained inextricably linked to it over time, even though they had not been designed specifically as a means of describing its content. They were an essential complement to it, enriching it with meaning, modifying it and contributing a language that could be traced back to the same artistic context.

This was especially true of the punk and New Wave movement, which was among the last musical movements in which records were still closely linked to their covers. Using these premises as its starting point, *Outside the Lines* aims to take a new angle, looking at a selection of the most significant album covers and revisiting them through the working material produced during the photo shoots that created them.

The time frame of the images chosen for inclusion in *Outside the Lines* runs from 1976 to 1982 – years during which punk and New Wave

Inascoltable
Skiantos
Harpo's Music
1977

Sire Records
1977–1978

took on the shape of something broader than just a musical movement, despite the fact that they contained opposing and contradictory visions. Embracing as they did a wide range of disciplines, from music to graphic design, photography, poetry and live performance, they came to represent an attitude, an aesthetic approach and a veritable artistic *avant-garde*, which took different forms depending on geographical location and artistic context.

The arguments and confusion that treated the terms 'punk' and 'New Wave' as if they were contrasting, denoting separate musical movements, helped to create a view of this multifaceted artistic world that was too partial and – in our opinion – not comprehensive enough.

On this point, it is worth noting that 'New Wave' was used initially by Sire Records in the United States as a marketing device to flag up newly contracted bands such as the Talking Heads and the Ramones. Lifted straight from French – a direct translation of the term *nouvelle vague* – it had a more intellectual sound and sat well with the anti-commercial image being promoted for these bands, which were considered experimental and for which a 'trashy' label such as 'punk' would not have been a good fit.

In 1970s Britain, where the public was relatively easy to shock, 'New Wave' was used to describe the music of bands that weren't exactly punk but were linked to the same musical scene, in order to distinguish them from other bands that were considered offensive or even banned from Britain. British New Wave bands had a more sophisticated attitude; they were sometimes musically more refined, and their ideas and politics seemed less committed.

As far as the British and US press were concerned the two terms were only briefly interchangeable, from 1976 to 1977. Already by late 1977 (despite a relentless media campaign by Malcolm McLaren) New Wave had replaced 'punk' to describe new underground music in the UK. In 1978, punk – in the sense of a label that described a movement – imploded. In media interviews at the time, many groups refused to be described as punk.

In a short time it had become an inconvenient word, which conjured up a negative image that was deemed unhelpful in the record industry.

It is our view that, during the period when the album covers chosen for *Outside the Lines* were produced, the terms were inseparable. These were the most important years of New Wave and punk in the musical sphere and, with hindsight, all those bands that were more or less part of it can be classed together, despite an apparent lack of stylistic unity.

After 1982, styles began to degenerate. New Wave and punk, which at their birth had contained many contrasting characteristics and were hard to reduce to a single definition, began to disintegrate and branch off in different directions. On the one hand, they gravitated towards the musical mainstream and the fashion industry, where they gave rise to a succession of fetishes and clones that have been reworked right up to the present day. On the other, they exploded into a gigantic and vigorously growing number of DIY movements, which gave rise to a multitude of by-products that came together anew in what came to be called indie music – itself, in turn, commercialized and absorbed into the mainstream.

In parallel with this vigorous growth in record production, a series of circumstances, chiefly due to global technological developments, was to banish the album cover to an ever more marginal role in the recording world.

In 1982, in a factory in Hannover, Germany, Philips produced the first commercial CD – a recording of *Eine Alpensinfonie* (*An Alpine Symphony*) by Richard Strauss, performed by the Berlin Philharmonic under the baton of Herbert von Karajan. And although the first pop album produced in CD form was *The Visitors* by the Swedish group Abba, the first to be commercially released was Billy Joel's *52nd Street*, which went on sale in Japan at the same time as the first CD player – on 1 October 1982.

With its 12-cm (4¾-in) square format, the CD diminished the importance of the album cover as an image. Old vinyl recordings – whose images had been conceived for album covers that were 30-cm (12-in) square – were reissued in a format one-third of the original size!

Although over the years adaptation to the small format and various approaches to packaging have sought to endow the CD cover with greater visual impact, such ploys have failed to reproduce the aesthetic power that LP covers exerted on behalf of the vinyl object they contained. Technology moved on very rapidly from CDs to downloadable digital music, the ubiquitous end product we all know today.

This book comes at a point in time when the album cover has ceased to have aesthetic importance. And it takes a reversed perspective – pushing the finished images into the background and, in their place, giving voice to unused shots, failed attempts and discarded material. Thanks to original material made available by photographers, these discarded offcuts have become the protagonists in this fascinating account of the birth of images which, over time, have become icons of an era.

The material shown here comes from the archives of 30 photographers who worked with some of the most interesting punk and New Wave bands. They include working prints made by the photographers themselves for consideration for album covers, or simply to be filed – and, most exciting of all, reproductions of contact prints made during photo shoots. Separated out and enlarged, these offer an invaluable

The Semantics Of Punk
Twisted fanzine #3

testimony of the work on location of well-known music photographers of the time – such as Gered Mankowitz, who shot musicians at the start of their careers, including a very young Billy Idol, immortalized in 1978 on the cover of Generation X's first album, and the still little-known Annie Lennox, photographed for the cover of the Tourists' *Reality Effect*, released in 1979.

The sequences of frames, like strips of film for a video clip that was never shot, show poses, viewpoints or simply details that differ from the shot on the cover, offering a unique glimpse of the way these professionals prepare their sets, create poses and interact with an artist. They have the power to bring him or her back to life, revealing details – such as a grimace or a different way of looking at the lens – that had remained hidden and, in this way, manage to give new life to that wonderful musical receptacle that was the vinyl record.

Seen in this very special way, cult objects, such as the cover of David Bowie's *Heroes*, the work of Masayoshi Sukita in 1977, or the image with the famous refrigerator of the Cure's album *Three Imaginary Boys*, shot by Martyn Goddard in 1979, emerge from their static state of commercial icons, acquiring not one but many possible other lives, offering us the opportunity to witness their gestation before they became fixed into what we know today.

Outside the Lines is first and foremost a selection of photographs. It is not meant to be a piece of systematic research or a catalogue of the musicians and bands of the punk and New Wave era – partly because many covers of albums regarded as pivotal were created using elaborate graphics. Neither have the albums been chosen because of their musical value; in this case they are images first and music second.

In choosing them we have kept an open mind, eschewing preconceived dogmas and labels. Instead, we have focused on those covers whose images displayed a particular attitude to punk, and which showed some stylistic parallels as well as possessing an intrinsic aesthetic value. The selection traces two distinct threads that cover the period from 1976 to 1982 in the US and in the UK.

The first chapter – 1, 2, 3, 4! The American Wave – opens with a cover by Bob Gruen for *Max's Kansas City*, an album featuring various artists which came out in 1976, and ends with the photographs Esther Friedman shot for Iggy Pop's *Zombie Birdhouse* (1982).

The US section is introduced by a key image of the birth of New Wave – a true piece of history – although I doubt that Bob Gruen was aware, when he pressed the shutter release, of how important the event he was immortalizing was to become.

The photograph shows a group of people on a New York street, outside a club. It's not an especially interesting image from an aesthetic

Generation X (first)
Generation X
Chrysalis
1978

or compositional point of view; but it is interesting for its content because it is a commentary, in part, on the LP's contents. For in among the crowd you can see the musicians who play on it: Wayne County, Cherry Vanilla and Suicide. Moreover, the club is the very same Max's Kansas City, a nightclub and restaurant at 213 Park Avenue South, an historic meeting place for musicians, poets, artists and politicians in the 1960s and 1970s, and the scene of those early concerts. This is an exceptional document and everything that appears in the picture constitutes a very powerful bomb that is about to explode – the fuse has just been lit!

The US thread continues with images that trace the progressive transformation – both musical and aesthetic – of New Wave and punk.

Its starting point is two bands photographed by Roberta Bayley: the Ramones and the Heartbreakers. Posed in front of a wall, they look perfect – they say all they need to say; they represent a true beginning, something that needs to be portrayed just as it is, without too much context or added frills. We see the same approach – the search for an image that suits musicians who needed, above all, to be recognized for what they were – in the *modus operandi* of Edo Bertoglio. The three surviving shots taken by him for the cover of Blondie's *Parallel Lines* appear in this book. So too with Ebet Roberts' work for Suicide – he used the same process as George DuBose did for the cover of the B-52's album, pasting cut-out silhouettes of the musicians on to a yellow background. It should be pointed out though that DuBose, a true experimenter, obtained this result only after venturing to use Mylar®, a reflective material of which he was very fond. However, in the case of the B-52's, the resulting image may have been deemed too suggestive of psychedelic experience and was therefore modified.

It's clear from the interplay of lights and mirrors he created for his work with Lydia Lunch that DuBose was rarely satisfied with a simple, unadorned subject in front of his lens. Here, the doubling of the singer's image is so precise and clean that it is difficult to distinguish the real one from the reflection – the end result being a focus on the doubled image.

Another interesting experiment is the one carried out by Martyn Goddard on Blondie's face, for the second, picture-disc edition of *Parallel Lines*, produced in 1978. A curious series of frames leads us into the very middle of the set for the photo shoot. That day, at the Gramercy Park Hotel, Debbie Harry was photographed in all the preliminary phases of a photo shoot, from make-up to relaxing with other group members, and finally the creative phase proper, before she was immortalized in one of the most captivating shots out of the thousands taken during her singing career.

Parallel Lines
Blondie
Chrysalis
1978

In a totally different key is the compositional simplicity of the close-ups Seth Tillett took of Lizzy Mercier Descloux. Although many photographs taken in the world of music are the result of collaboration between two artists – photographer and musician – where the personality of each comes through as a discrete entity, in these portraits Seth Tillett casts an introspective gaze over his model that suggests, in a veiled way, a harmonious, almost intimate, relationship between the two. The thoughtful expression that brings out Lizzy Mercier Descloux's strange beauty is true and natural – not the result of an artificially constructed pose. We see the same immediacy and naturalness in the photograph shot in the street in New York, which, thanks to an apparently casual composition combined with questionable image quality, makes her look extremely punk.

The early 1980s saw a change of style and greater care taken in the preparation of sets. The clearest demonstration of this are the images of the car crashing into the swimming pool put together by Rod Swenson for the Plasmatics.

The second chapter, New Wave and the first British LPs, restarts from year zero with the cover of the first punk record produced in the UK: *Damned Damned Damned*, photographed by Peter Kodick (Peter Gravelle), and an image with an exquisitely British flavour. The photographs chosen for this section are generally more polished images, which certainly involved more work in the studio. However, they have managed to retain that aura that distinguishes New Wave, incorporating all its ingredients. They exploit the 'poseur' attitudes of the musicians, who wear leather blousons, PVC raincoats, hand-coloured T-shirts, or ties and white shirts combined with worn-out jackets. They flaunt short hair and the very first mohicans, and make use of accessories that will become iconic, such as safety pins, badges and chains around the neck.

From a strictly photographic point of view, much use is made of black and white, which is close to the DIY ethos. This approach was taken by Chris Gabrin, Martyn Goddard, Chalkie Davies and Brian Griffin, who shot album covers for Elvis Costello, the Jam, the Specials, the Pretenders and Joe Jackson. Alongside black and white, there was juxtaposition of lurid and complementary colours, often intensely heightened, with sometimes more provocative effects than those encountered on the US scene. One of the most striking examples – among many – is the cover that Andy Earl made in 1981 for Bow Wow Wow's *See Jungle! See Jungle! Go Join Your Gang Yeah, City All Over! Go Ape Crazy!*, which was considered one of the finest in the history of vinyl – aside from the scandal it created. Like a true contemporary Édouard Manet, as in his painting *Déjeuner sur l'herbe*, Earl had Annabella Lwin, the band's 15-year-old-singer, pose nude.

Damned Damned Damned
The Damned
Stiff Records
1977

As the title of this chapter suggests, it is focused largely on British musicians as well as featuring a handful of bands of other nationalities, such as Japanese: Yellow Magic Orchestra, with Ryuichi Sakamoto at the start of his career, 'robotized' by Masayoshi Sukita, whose strident, starkly contrasting colours proclaim a musical product that is cold, electronic and new. Jim Rakete's image of Nina Hagen, on the other hand, returns to a simple style much closer to the early Americans, almost as if the aim was to emphasize the fact that that product belonged to this new kind of music, despite the geographic and cultural distance separating the singer – who roguishly evokes German cabaret of the inter-war years.

From a musical point of view, to place a singer such as David Bowie in this context may seem like stretching the point – even though it's well known that there was cross-fertilization between Bowie and Iggy Pop, who were close friends and, at the time, were both staying in Berlin. The cover of *Heroes*, photographed by Sukita, is perfectly in line stylistically with the images Brian Griffin and Keith Collie shot for Lene Lovich and Ultravox. These are cold images, based on contrived, unnatural, almost robotic poses, totally in keeping with the musical transformation that was taking place: a moving away from simple, fast-moving early rock 'n' roll towards refined, synthetic electronic sounds, inspired by east European atmospheres and clearly influenced by Kraftwerk.

It is fascinating to observe the singular way in which Lene Lovich worked on her own image. On the cover of *Stateless* (US edition, 1978), shot by Brian Griffin, the singer appears in an elegant grey suit, almost military in style, and her syncopated, robotic movements suggest the heroine of a totalitarian science-fiction future, inspired by Fritz Lang's film *Metropolis*, George Orwell's novel *Nineteen Eighty-Four* or by intrigue at the court of some central European country in the early 20th century.

In *Flex*, shot by the same photographer in 1979, a different character comes on the scene, displaying completely different visual characteristics: long braids, ample skirts, the veils and lace typical of clothes in a bygone age, shawls and earrings. Such features restore a feminine image with a strong personality, but also one with cultural connotations – a mixture of gypsy woman and traditional witch.

All this against a background of heterogeneous signs, starting with lyrics full of references to magic – where there appear crystal balls, cabbalistic numbers, telepathic forces and rebellious, stateless characters, the gypsies of the future.

The cover of Ultravox's album is a comment on itself, together with its title: *Vienna*.

Two covers from 1982 bring to a close the timeline of these images, held together by that very slender, sometimes invisible, connecting

Heroes
David Bowie
RCA Victor
1977

thread that goes by the name of New Wave and punk. Both dispense with showing the musicians' faces. For Bauhaus's *Press the Eject and Give Me the Tape*, Eugene Merinov shot a close-up of Peter Murphy completely hidden by a cymbal, while in the metaphysical landscape portrayed by Brian Griffin for Depeche Mode's *A Broken Frame*, the three musicians have simply vanished into nothingness.

This is the symptom of the aesthetic degeneration that New Wave was to experience from this point onwards. The crude image of a musician was no longer enough to convey it.

The year 1982 did not mark the end of an era – only of the story of that explosion whose fuse had been lit a few years earlier in New York; the bomb exploded, but its fragments are still raining down on us from the sky today.

Stateless
Lene Lovich
Stiff Records
1978

Author **Glenn O'Brien**

Title # De–Picted!

In fashion photography, if you work for American *Vogue*, you have made it.

A friend of mine who is a famous fashion photographer, and who has a somewhat lesser-known but highly accomplished art career, told me that he wouldn't work for American *Vogue*, the most famous and powerful fashion magazine in the world. But that's the big time, I said, why would you not work for *Vogue*? He answered that when he worked for Italian *Vogue*, if he had 12 pages he handed them 12 prints. American *Vogue* asked for all the film. 'I can't give you all the film; I've got to edit,' he told them. 'I gave them at least ten frames of each shot. They insisted on more. I wouldn't give it. Finally I threw it all out. That was my first and last *Vogue* shoot. In photography only half of it is taking the shot. The other is picking it, editing.'

This fact has driven many of the photographers I know to the verge of madness since digital photography has become standard – at least in fashion and commercial photography. In fashion it used to be that the model emerged from hair and make-up and the photographer grabbed a camera, shot a roll and an assistant handed over another loaded camera, and then he probably shot another roll and another until the moment was gone and model and photographer, temporarily exhausted, looked positively post-coital, as in the film *Blow-Up*, which launched an entire generation of heterosexual fashion photographers.

But that kind of sexy frenzy of posing and shooting is obsolete. Today the model emerges made-up and styled, and the photographer takes a snap and instantly the frame is displayed on a large video monitor, and it is immediately assessed by the client or the fashion editor. Now the photographer is the guy who aims the camera and pushes the shutter. There's no heat. No energy. You might as well be shooting a car or a layer cake. The transition to digital photography has probably been a little less traumatic for the rock 'n' roll photographer, a profession that is a strange hybrid of fashion photographer, combat photographer, fan, psychiatrist, diplomat, scene-maker, sometimes musician wannabe and sometimes groupie. But of course now the star can see every frame on the video screen as it clicks out of the camera, so the contact sheet has still lost its privacy and its mystique. No, rock 'n' roll photography isn't what it used to be either. It's not just the digital democratization and demotion of the role of the photographer; it's simply not so important.

Once upon a time not so long ago the album cover was absolutely crucial in making a record successful. The world was not as saturated with image as it is today. The long-playing album sleeve, all 30cm x 30cm (12 x 12in) of it, was quite simply the face of the band. When it was successful, the cover shot was a true icon that distilled the personality of the artist and their music into a single contagious hieroglyph.

In some cases you could argue that the photographer was one of the most important players in the making of a hit – often demonstrably more crucial than the bass player.

This volume is an unusual study in rock 'n' roll photography because it's not so much about the iconic shot but the alternate shots, about the process. This isn't a study of the headliners from the contact sheet, but the opening acts. The pictures not used provide a fascinating perspective, giving us insight on the period of punk and New Wave, but also a sense of how iconography functions and the power that images have over our perceptions.

We contemplate the cover shot by Masayoshi Sukita of David Bowie's 1977 *Heroes*, with Bowie, seemingly entranced, making a cryptic, mystical hand gesture, and we wonder how differently we might have taken the music if a less strange shot had been selected. Here is an original contact sheet with 9 frames – all of them interesting, quirky and peculiar – but none of them seems possible in retrospect. But that's knowing what we know now. How much did that single shot add to the mystique of the songs? Enough that it now seems fated. Enough that it caused *The Next Day* 36 years later. That photo embodies the inevitable.

Looking at the visual signifiers of the music from three or four decades ago, you have to be struck by how modern they look now. This is a past that could pass for the future. We could say, well, of course they had to have big photos to sell those huge discs. The most noticeable difference between these musical visions and those of today, aside from the fact that there's less nudity, is that there seems to be a broader spectrum of individuality here in the past. We don't see the heavy hand of fashion and branding. We see characters, playing parts that they wrote for themselves, being themselves, inventing themselves. Perhaps that's why there seems to be a stronger brand of portraiture here, but what is portraiture but an inspired look at personality? Maybe punk or New Wave or whatever you call it was an aberrant explosion of personality, but it's funny how it holds up. Maybe personality is something that it's worth having a crisis over. It's something that comes from the artists and it can't be tacked on by the company, the stylist or the curator.

So what can we learn here? Maybe we should go for something original, not fashionable. Maybe we should keep the company man off the shoot and off our back. Maybe we can learn to not take the first selfie that comes along but take a long, hard look at the contact sheets of our lives. Yeah, that one is really handsome, but that one is really weird. What's that about? If you're lucky, they'll still be wondering about that shot in 40 years.

Author **George DuBose**

Title # Punk!

punk |pʌŋk|
noun
1 informal, a worthless person (often used as a general term of abuse).
• a criminal or hoodlum.
• derogatory (in prison slang) a passive male homosexual.
• an inexperienced young person; a novice.
• a short piece of hemp rope with a burning end used to light cannons on sailing ships when it was too windy to use anything else.
• camel dung on a skewer used to light fireworks
2 (also **punk rock**) a loud, fast-moving and aggressive form of rock music, popular in the late 1970s and early 1980s.
• (also **punk rocker**) an admirer or player of such music, typically characterized by coloured, spiked hair and clothing decorated with safety pins or zippers.
3 soft, crumbly wood that has been attacked by fungus, sometimes used as tinder.

adjective
1 informal, in poor or bad condition: I felt too punk to eat.
2 of or relating to punk rock and its associated subculture: a punk band | a punk haircut.

verb
1 to trick someone: I was punked by my brother's friends; they really fooled me this time.

DERIVATIVES
punkish *adjective*
punky *adjective*

ORIGIN late 17th century. (sense 3): perhaps, in some senses, related to archaic punk [prostitute], also to spunk.

Punks are born that way. One can't become a punk by design. Alexander was a great punk. Genghis Khan, Attila, Henry VIII, Napoleon, Mozart, Elvis were all punks of their time.

One cannot call oneself a punk. It is more than an attitude or a fashion style; it is a philosophy. It is an impression you leave with someone else. Calling someone a punk used to be derogatory or inflammatory. It has become a term of respect for an independent, anarchistic way of life roughly associated with a musical style and peripheral lifestyle.

My first exposure to punk rock was in 1976. I went to CBGBs for the first time, not knowing what to expect. I paid my $3 cover and saw the band Television on stage. My first impression was that the guitar player was playing worse than I would. I had long forgone dreams of being a professional guitarist and just didn't understand why this guitar player (Tom Verlaine) was making such a public attempt to be so bad... so bad that I went back to the doorman and asked for my money back.

I had never heard of punk rock. I soon learned that even accomplished musicians were unlearning their technique, stripping songs to the bone. Punk gave rise to the concept that serious musical study was unnecessary, even undesirable. Primitive, raw and minimal music, vocals as an instrument, obscured lyrics – all that mattered was the power and emotion of the performance.

Later, I saw Lydia Lunch and Teenage Jesus And The Jerks open for the New York debut of the B-52's at Max's Kansas City. I heard Lydia complaining backstage that one of their songs was too long at 45 seconds and that song needed to be cut to 30 seconds. I finally began to understand about punk rock. Lydia's band was trying to play poorly, the B-52's were playing as well as they could.

I hated Teenage Jesus And The Jerks and loved the B's. I made both of their debut album covers. Go fuck yourself figure...

1, 2, 3, 4!

The American Wave

Bob Gruen

Max's Kansas City

Various Artists

1976

Max's Kansas City is a sort of postcard from the cultural transformation that was under way in New York in 1976, bringing together an interesting mix of sounds. The performers were all regulars at the evening sessions held at Max's Kansas City restaurant and club. One in particular stands out from the rest: Wayne County, who since 1972 had been playing in the pioneering proto-punk band Queen Elizabeth. He was a multi-talented artist – stage actor, musician, subversive, and transsexual; a threatening and vulgar provocateur – who played himself in various underground films.

Wayne County was a DJ at Max's, whose atmosphere and clientele he knew well. 'Max's Kansas City' is the compilation's opening track, featuring instructive lyrics that tell all about the club and its regular clients – a sort of advertising jingle in the style of Lou Reed, lasting 5:38 minutes. Wayne County's tale is rounded off by the Fast, Harry Toledo, Pere Ubu, Cherry Vanilla, John Collins Band and Suicide, in a pot-pourri of acerbic sounds foreshadowing the new scene.

The back of the album cover reads: 'Now you can share in this new exciting scene! Give this record a listen and you'll know why the crowds are going wild at Max's.'

Bob Gruen: *Tommy Dean, owner of Max's, called me and asked me to shoot the cover of his 'Live at Max's' album. Peter Crowley, who booked the bands at Max's, arranged to meet in front of the club on a Sunday afternoon with all the groups on the record there. It was probably the only time everyone saw each other in the daylight. I set my camera on a tripod on the planter on the divider in the middle of Park Avenue and had the bands arrange themselves on the sidewalk in front of the club. It only took about an hour to set up and take the photos.*

Max's Kansas City
Various Artists
Ram Records
1976

max's
kansas city
eak chick
oster peas
NO PARKING
max's
kansas city
max's
upstairs at max's
THE

Roberta Bayley

Ramones

The Ramones

1976

This album was recorded in seven days, and issued in February 1976. It had cost just $6,000 – an extremely modest budget for one of the greatest and most significant records in the history of music.

It contains 14 tracks on just 2 sides of vinyl – some of them lasting little more than a minute, and the longest just 2½ minutes.

Half an hour of stark sounds, with guitar recorded on one channel, bass on the other and drums on both. In comparison to the pop rock albums of the time, it could have been considered an 'ugly duckling' – and indeed on its release it didn't meet with the commercial success it was to enjoy in the following years.

What's beyond question is that – thanks to its cover image of four musicians who are decidedly not 'star' material, its peculiar structure, which was unique for the time, and the subjects of its songs – it must be considered the ultimate concept punk album.

Roberta Bayley: The Ramones' first album cover is probably my most well-known image, along with the photo of Joey Ramone carrying a surfboard on the beach. Punk magazine had featured the Ramones in issue number one (Lou Reed was on the cover) in 1976 and was putting them on the cover of issue number three. In February 1976, John Holmstrom and Legs McNeil set up a photo session with the band at Arturo Vega's loft on East Second Street (now named Joey Ramone Place). The Ramones asked for a different photographer, but Holmstrom stuck by me. The photos inside the loft weren't very interesting, so we went outside and came across a playground a few yards from Arturo's loft. I shot two rolls of film outside and the twelfth frame on the roll was the album cover! It was the 28th roll of film I shot as a professional – how wild is that? It was a fast shoot, everyone was relaxed. No one knew it would be the album cover. It was only after the band saw the photographs of the professional photographer Sire Records had hired that they got into a panic because the record was about to come out. Danny Fields was calling around, desperate for an image. Sire chose mine. I got $125.

Ramones
The Ramones
Sire Records
1976

A →8 →8A →9 →9A →10

A →14 →14A →15 →15A →16

19A →20 →20A →21A →22

→ 11   → 11A   → 12   → 12A   → 13   →
KODAK SAFETY FILM 5063   KODAK SAFETY FILM 5063

AFETY FILM 5063   → 17   → 17A   → 18   → 18A   → 19   →
KODAK SAFETY FILM 5063   KODAK SAFETY

→ 23   → 23A   → 24   → 24A   → 25   →
KODAK SAFETY FILM 5063   KODAK SAFETY FILM 5063

Photographer	# Roberta Bayley
Album	# L.A.M.F.
Artist	# Heartbreakers
Year	# 1977

Although it met with criticism because of its questionable sound quality, this album remains an immensely important product of the punk movement. Recorded in February 1977 but issued only in October of that year, it went through a complex post-production phase because of dissatisfaction and mutual misunderstandings. Its 12 tracks were remixed several times, and more than 300 mixings were recorded. Each member of the Heartbreakers suggested their own provisional version; each mixing was considered and each was discarded amid the utter indecision of the engineers and the musicians themselves.

Beyond this, it became apparent that the sound problems with Track Records' original version of *L.A.M.F.* were attributable to the poor quality of the vinyl used for the pressing.

Roberta Bayley: Leee Black Childers, the Heartbreakers' manager, called and asked me to shoot the album cover for the band. Leee was a fantastic photographer, but he was in London and the band was in New York, so Leee hired me. I went down to their rehearsal space around Crosby Street, and I shot about five–six rolls of film, all in colour, all with flash – not my usual style; I prefer shooting in daylight. We took the film over to a lab and got it processed in a few hours and the band and I looked at all the slides on a projector and narrowed it down to four–five images. It's always hard to get all the members of a band to agree, but they finally did, and Walter Lure got the pictures overnighted to Leee in London. That became the cover of the L.A.M.F. album. The poster of that image was plastered all over London at one point. I love that photo so much. The Heartbreakers had a falling out with their label Track Records – I believe they actually broke into the record company's office and stole the master tapes. I never got paid, but one day in 1977, the day before I was heading back to New York, I ran into Leee on Oxford Street in London. He pulled out $300 and gave it to me – hey, that was more than twice what Sire paid for the Ramones cover.

L.A.M.F.
Heartbreakers
Track Records
1977

Edo Bertoglio
Parallel Lines
Blondie
1978

Sophisticated, caustic and modern, Blondie were essentially synonymous with their vocalist, the strikingly blonde Debbie Harry, one of the most powerful female icons of the 1970s and, probably, the most beautiful rock singer of all time.

Parallel Lines proved to be a highly successful album for Blondie, but it was also one that made a clean break with the past. While their debut album featured rich, though acerbic, sounds and their second album, *Plastic Letters*, displayed effective pop rock, this 1978 album deliberately chose a light pop idiom, with a sprinkling of New Wave. At all events, it passed muster. Whether thanks to its producer, Mike Chapman, a wizard of 1970s commercial pop, a successful UK tour in 1978 or simply the ever more captivating presence of Debbie Harry, *Parallel Lines* sold extremely well (an estimated 20 million copies to date). It shot to number one in the British charts, number two in the Canadian albums chart, and number six in the US top LPs rankings. It sits in 140th place in *Rolling Stone*'s 'The 500 Greatest Albums of All Time'.

Parallel Lines already displays the signs of what Blondie were to become in the 1980s: from this point onwards, they embraced a progressively more commercial sound, even going so far as to flirt with disco-wave, as in the later (and widely acclaimed) 'Call Me'.

Perhaps they unwittingly created one of the most successful genres of the 1970s – the 'disco-punk' that was to influence entire generations of synth-pop groups and others too. Be that as it may, this album – which on a first hearing may appear banal, but isn't – remains a genuine piece of work and contains at least two historic and essential tracks.

Edo Bertoglio: *When Chris Stein asked me to do the cover of* Parallel Lines *he mentioned that he had already done some work with another photographer (which turned out to be Roberta Bayley, but this didn't come out until a few years later). He asked me if I agreed to do it for $500, seeing as they had already used up much of the budget. I said okay and we went ahead with the photo that was used.*

Parallel Lines
Blondie
Chrysalis
1978

Martyn Goddard

<u>**Parallel Lines picture disc**</u>

Blondie

1978

A limited-edition picture-disc version of *Parallel Lines* was also issued, featuring the famous photograph of Debbie Harry licking a vinyl LP.

Martyn Goddard: The Parallel Lines *picture-disc image was from a session I organized to produce an image for the cover of the* Telegraph Magazine *in the UK. It was shot in Debbie's hotel suite in the Gramercy Park Hotel. I had the image in my head before leaving England and had obtained a vinyl white label test pressing album from Chrysalis Records – my plan being to ask Ms Harry to kiss the blank LP. She was totally up for the concept but my second request I thought might be trickier. It happened to be London Fashion Week in New York while I was in New York, and a hair stylist working on the shows I had worked on back in the UK agreed to produce a special hairstyle for the shoot. To my surprise, Debbie agreed, the time was set, the stylist arrived but at the last minute Debbie decided her hair was in terrible condition – not fit for a photo session! After ten minutes with the stylist, he sorted the situation and we were go again. I set about building a small studio in the sitting room using just one portable flash unit, a stand, tripod and my trusty Nikon FM.*

The close-up part of the shoot progressed quickly and I was able to produce not only the cover for the magazine – on seeing the results of the shoot, Peter Wagg, the art director at the record company, chose one of the outtakes for Blondie's European picture-disc version of the great Parallel Lines *album.*

Later that week I travelled with the group to Philadelphia, when they were the support band for Alice Cooper, and enjoyed photographing the band's live one-off gig at the Palladium in New York. In June I arrived at the studio for the first photo session for their record company Chrysalis, one of several planned for the week; I could sense a tense atmosphere. As a photographer, shooting in recording studios was always a problem on a technical level, with period camera equipment and film stock, in what were very dark, functional spaces. Additionally, one had to work around the process of recording a record. It was soon evident that Blondie, and Debbie Harry, in particular, were having issues with record producer Mike Chapman.

Parallel Lines picture disc
Blondie
Chrysalis
1978

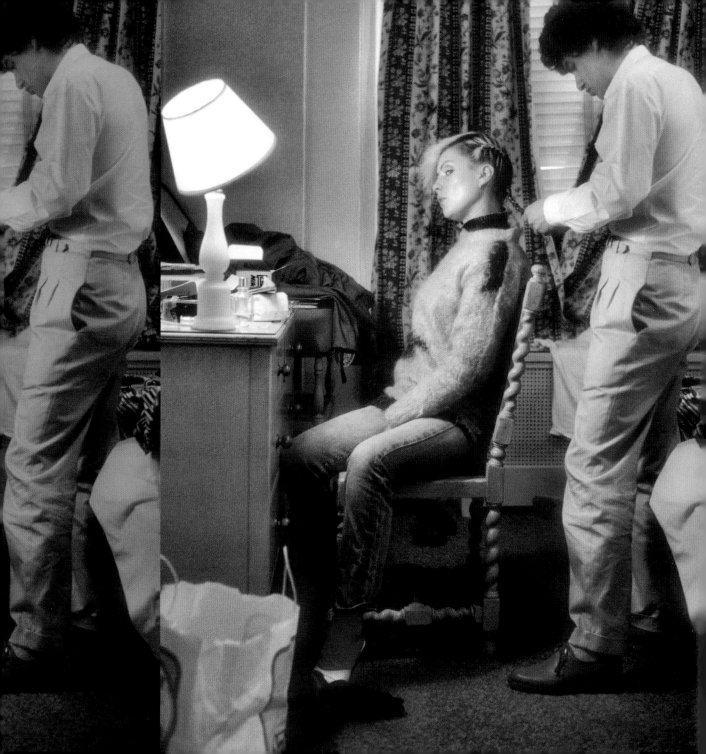

Photographer	**Esther Friedman**
Album	**TV Eye: Live 1977**
Artist	**Iggy Pop**
Year	**1978**

This was a quick and painless way out of the contract with RCA, which had previously issued *The Idiot* and *Lust for Life*, two discs that had caused a great stir but hadn't sold particularly well. For this reason, the label offered their artist an expedient way to end their relationship without wasting too much energy or investing too much creativity. It's said that Iggy Pop was offered an advance of $90,000 and a commission for a live album as a means of terminating the contract. *TV Eye: Live 1977* is an album put together by assembling some tapes of live performances, which had been hastily tidied up in a German studio by Iggy himself. It contains extracts from recordings of concerts at The Agora in Cleveland, Ohio, and the Aragon in Chicago, Illinois, in March 1977, and at the Uptown Theater in Kansas City, Missouri, in October that year. In terms of quality, the disc is little better than a bootleg recording.

TV Eye: Live 1977
Iggy Pop
RCA
1978

Photographer	**William Christie**
Album	**Venus D'Vinyl**
Artist	**Cherry Vanilla**
Year	**1979**

This page shows Kathleen Dorritie, stage name Cherry Vanilla, before she became a singer, at her theatre debut in Andy Warhol's *Pork*, where she played Amanda Pork alongside Jayne County in the role of Vulva.

In the early 1970s she worked at Mainman Ltd as an advertising agent for David Bowie. She was famous for her shocking marketing strategies, and would start her radio advertisements by declaring: 'Hi, my name is Cherry Vanilla and I've got scoops for you...' She created a furore when she offered oral sex to any DJ who had played one of Bowie's records.

In 1974 Cherry Vanilla formed a band with Kasim Sulton; later, in 1976 came Cherry Vanilla & Her Staten Island Band. Her poems for the book *Pop Tart* date from the same year.

She was part of the first small group of young London punks. September 1977 saw the release of her single 'The Punk', followed in February 1978 by her debut album, *Bad Girl*. After the release of her second, *Venus D'Vinyl*, she returned to the US.

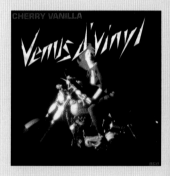

Venus D'Vinyl
Cherry Vanilla
RCA Victor
1979

Photographer **George DuBose**

Album **The B-52's**

Artist **The B-52's**

Year **1979**

Originally from Athens, Georgia, the band frequented Max's in New York as early as 1977. Their photographer, George DuBose, described meeting them there on 12 December that year, along with Teenage Jesus And The Jerks. In 1979 the producer Chris Blackwell insisted on recording an album almost entirely live, without overdubbing, to capture as closely as possible the sound quality and energy of the group's live performances. As well as their own numbers, the B-52's produced provocative covers of easy-listening classics by Henry Mancini, Petula Clark and Tony Hatch, in the process creating an unusual and unique product. The album is a mixture of frenetic rock 'n' roll, dance music, and surf music.

George DuBose: *I had the idea to produce a 16- x 20-in [40- x 50-cm] poster in black and white to 'snipe' around the clubs, where the band would be playing. I didn't know about wheat paste, and after I had stapled posters around the block where Max's Kansas City was and got back the point where I started, all the posters were gone. After that I began selling the posters for 52 cents or two for a dollar.*

Interview magazine published the picture with Glenn O'Brien's interview. Two years later, the band had just been signed by Chris Blackwell of Island Records. I got a phone call from Tony Wright, the creative director of Island Records, who wanted to see all of my shots of the B-52's. When I got to his office, it was obvious that the band had already decided on using this picture. Tony asked me if he could hand-colour it. We changed the Mylar® balloon that Kate was holding to matching shoes and handbag that I had bought her in a thrift shop. Tony asked me how much money I wanted for use of the shot. I told him I had no idea. He offered me $750, which I quickly calculated as five weeks of my present pay. Tony hated the group and used the name of 'Sue Absurd' as his art-direction credit. It became one of our biggest covers and won many awards...

The B-52's
The B-52's
Warner Bros. Records
1979

Photographer	# Seth Tillett
Album	# Press Color
Artist	# Lizzy Mercier Descloux
Year	# 1979

The album *Press Color* came out in 1979. This time, Lizzy Mercier Descloux was billed as the main artist. Besides D J Barnes, the band included Erik Eliasson (formerly of Marie et les Garçons) on guitar, bass, drums and keyboards, Jimmie Young on drums and percussion, and other guest musicians. The music was more structured and richer – a mixture of funky disco and post-punk. Four of the album's eight tracks are covers: 'Mission Impossible' and 'Jim on the Move' by Lalo Schifrin, Arthur Brown's famous 'Fire' and 'Fever' by Peggy Lee, renamed 'Tumor' for the occasion (sadly, Lizzy was to die prematurely of a tumour). Despite its excellent quality, the disc did not meet with critical acclaim and struggled with distribution in the US, so much so that it was hard to find. This set a precedent that was to be repeated with all Lizzy's work.

Seth Tillett: *I tried for days to take a good picture of Lizzy. We even hired the great Serge Lutens to take a shot but nothing worked. Nothing showed her character or her strength. One night Lizzy and I looked at all the diapositives on a projector on the wall over our bed and then fell asleep, pretty frustrated. In the middle of the night I woke up, turned on the projector light with no slide, got my camera ready and woke Lizzy up. As soon as she sat up I took the cover shot. She was squinting into the bright light and it looked like a Soviet hero shot, from Eduard Tisse or Rodchenko, one of our favourites.*

Press Color
Lizzy Mercier Descloux
ZE Records
1979

Photographer **Julia Gorton**

Album # Pre Teenage Jesus And The Jerks

Artist # Teenage Jesus And The Jerks

Year # 1979

Raised in Rochester, in upstate New York, Lydia Lunch (real name Lydia Koch) often visited Manhattan to see punk performances. In 1976, aged 16, she moved to the Chelsea neighbourhood of New York City, not far from Max's Kansas City.

Lydia Lunch: *I wasn't thinking of setting up a band. Rather, I wanted to perform spoken poetry – I'd started writing at the age of 11. I wanted to get close to people through my poems, but the only person that was interested in me was Lenny Kaye [Patti Smith's guitarist]. Everyone else ran away.*

During those years Lydia Lunch met James Siegfried (aka James Chance, James White).

James Chance: *I had a small apartment between Avenue A and Second Street. One day she knocked on my door, saying she needed a place to stay, so I let her in. She showed me the songs she was writing, and I encouraged her to form a band. Lydia found a broken guitar, and decided that music could be a good vehicle for her poems.*

Lydia Lunch: *I couldn't play it, but I knew there was a sound that needed to come out from inside me – I needed to express what was driving me crazy. It wasn't a matter of having a band, of making music, but of having a different group of people from the usual, based on my primal anxiety, anger, hatred that would sow fear and panic in the audience. It had nothing to do with the classic, pleasant performance that would put people at their ease and entertain them. I wanted to create an atmosphere of repulsion. I was a teenage terrorist – what excited me was to destroy the tradition of melody and composition, and instead vent the horrible uproar of my internal torment in the most primitive way.*

The sound is rough, unpleasant; the music's rhythm is martial, minimal and obsessive, like a master whipping his slave.

Pre Teenage Jesus And
The Jerks
Teenage Jesus And The
Jerks
ZE Records
1979

Photographer **Julia Gorton**

Album **Teenage Jesus And The Jerks**

Artist **Teenage Jesus And The Jerks**

Year **1979**

James Chance: *Teenage Jesus were her expression; they were totally her band. At the time, we also played 'Jaded', a song written and sung by me. But she eliminated first the song, then me.*

Lydia Lunch: *I knew that James had another vision for the music, and he also liked to mix with the audience, which for me was taboo; I wanted to put barbed wire between the audience and us. Teenage were very cold, whereas James was a seething spirit. So he had to go.*

The music goes beyond the nihilism of punk and eliminates every rock 'n' roll element. The songs reflect a primitive but clearly disciplined approach of hammering minimalism that consists of repeated, fractured dissonances and cold, empty spaces where singing comes in. The sung passages are reminiscent of angry, childish echolalia, expressing 'need, fear and anger as uncontainable and contradictory impulses.'

Lydia Lunch: *A little is enough. That's what I think.*

Like discipline, or punishment.

You don't need 30 minutes of my music to understand what I'm talking about.

I've changed for myself… to amuse myself… That's the only reason. Teenage Jesus are the physical expression of me.

Teenage Jesus And The
Jerks
Teenage Jesus And The
Jerks
Migraine
1979

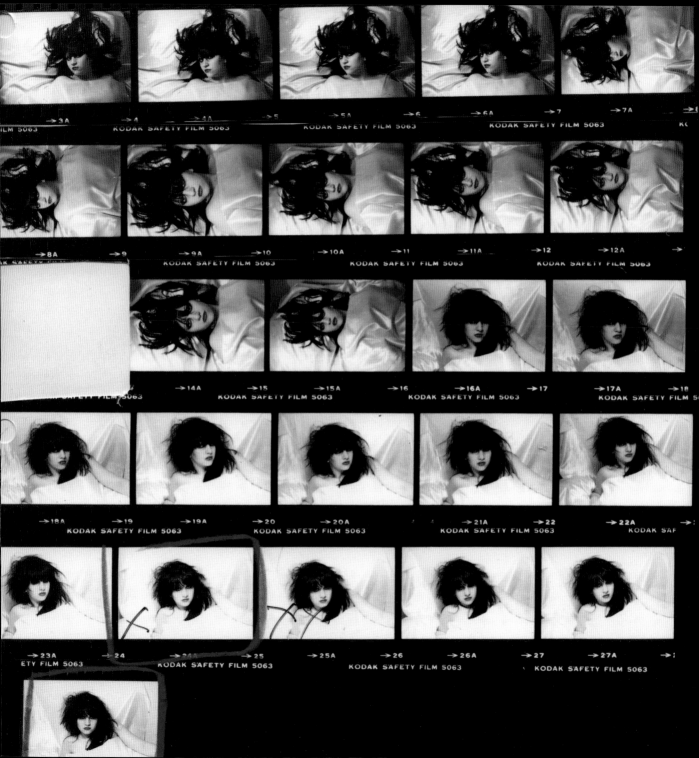

Photographer **George DuBose**

Album **Queen of Siam**

Artist **Lydia Lunch**

Year **1980**

The album *Queen of Siam* is a very polished production, with some superbly orchestrated passages. The singing voice doesn't shriek any more, but rather whispers in an oppressive way, with sighing murmurs. The disc is like a film noir, a cabaret, a macabre fairy tale.

It is a fascinating album, marked by the powerful femininity projected by its singer.

George Scott (aka Jack Ruby) and Robert Quine made a significant contribution to the disc, but most of the music was played by Pat Irwin.

Lunch: *I wanted to create this perverse, childish sound, and he succeeded in translating it into music for me...*

My new group is making an honest, fresh attempt to produce modern music, none of that pseudo-funk shit that many bands are doing, like the Contortions.

That's all old stuff, and funk should be left to funky folks. I don't like camp either – stuff like the B-52's, or rockabilly revival...

George DuBose: *When I got the contract to shoot Lydia for* Queen of Siam *from ZE Records, I asked Eric Boman, a* Vogue *fashion photographer, if he would do her hair and make-up. I was assisting Eric Boman at the time; he had just arrived in NYC from London where he had been the art director of British* Vogue*. I also knew that Eric didn't have a lot of money, so the fee from doing the hair and make-up for Lydia would be a help to him. After Eric spent a couple of hours fixing Lydia's hair and make-up, Eric asked her if she 'liked' it. She said, 'NO!' and proceeded to destroy the hairdo that Eric had done.*

The mirror idea was Lydia's. She showed me a book, Glamour Portraits of the '30s, *and in that book there was a portrait of Lucille Ball that she wanted me to copy. I prefer the images where the mirror is down flat like a table and she is looking into the mirror...*

Queen of Siam
Lydia Lunch
ZE Records
1980

Photographer **Brian Griffin**

Album **Soldier**

Artist **Iggy Pop**

Year **1980**

This was an album that did not enjoy as much success as its predecessors, perhaps because of the particularly affected and 'polished' image of Iggy Pop. Indeed, the disc made use of a large musical cast, including Glen Matlock (ex-Sex Pistols), Ivan Kral of Patti Smith Group, Klaus Krüger of Tangerine Dream, Steve New, guitarist with the Rich Kids, and Barry Andrews of XTC. Even the cover photo is by a big name – Brian Griffin – and the graphics are by the up-and-coming studio Rocking Russian, one of the most in-vogue names in music graphics at the time.

The new LP probably needed an image that was rougher, less well finished aesthetically and musically, and closer to the imaginary – to suit Iggy Pop's critics and fans.

It was to have been produced by James Williamson but, because of disagreements with David Bowie, who was taking part in an informal way in the recording sessions, the former member of the Stooges stepped down from the role. Bowie contributed a track, and his voice appears in a number of places. Here, yet again, the recording studio became a place where the two friends shared and exchanged ideas – with, in my view, excellent results.

Brian Griffin: *It was shot in a hired photographic studio in Notting Hill, London. I produced the background effect by spraying coloured paint around the shapes that the lights were producing.*

Soldier
Iggy Pop
Arista
1980

Boruch Alan Bermowitz, stage name Alan Vega, is best known for having been Suicide's vocalist. He began his career as a sculptor, becoming known for his 'light sculptures' – works made chiefly out of recycled materials.

In his Manhattan gallery, which was frequented by the New York Dolls, Television and Blondie, Alan Vega ran the Project of Living Artists, which was to create a certain amount of artistic ferment by encouraging fruitful cultural exchanges. It was there that he met the keyboard player Martin Rev, who from 1970 was to become his partner in the proto-punk duo Suicide. In 1980 the two split up to pursue solo careers.

In this LP and the following one, Vega continued to explore the rockabilly identity, which, in his earlier music-making, had been much more fragmented and less focused.

At the outset, the album was supposed to have been produced by Ric Ocasek, but in the end production passed to Chris Lord-Alge. This created problems for Vega during recording sessions – so much so that he claimed: 'They took all my songs and turned them into God knows what.'

Curtis Knapp: *Alan and Marty (Suicide) are very old friends and I made it a point to always be at their shows. By the time Alan was making his first solo record, I had changed from being an illustrator to a photographer. I had a studio on Union Square in New York City, where I photographed a few artists in the early '80s such as Madonna, REM, Andy Warhol and Alan Vega. Also I liked Alan's artwork he was working on at the time. Alan and Marty were always very nice friends to me and still are to this day.*

Alan Vega
Alan Vega
ZE Records
1980

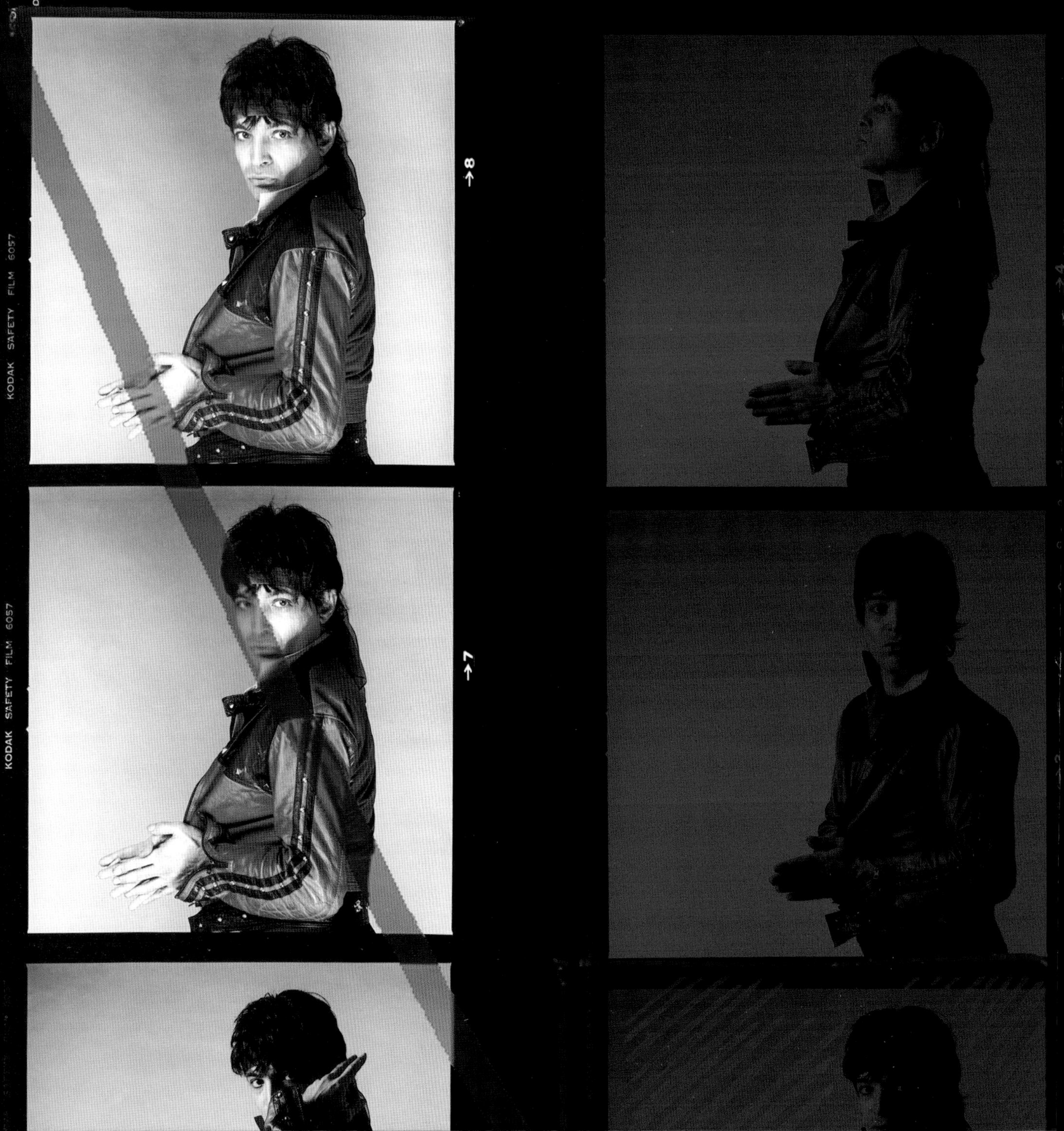
KODAK SAFETY FILM 6057
→8
KODAK SAFETY FILM 6057
→7

Photographer **Rod Swenson**

Album **New Hope for the Wretched**

Artist **Plasmatics**

Year **1980**

This album is unquestionably the forerunner of the hard-core punk scene that was to develop in the coming years.

Initially, production was to be the responsibility of Jimmy Miller, former producer of the Rolling Stones, but he was soon replaced by Rod Swenson, the manager, who looked after the album's conception, and by the sound engineer Ed Stasium.

As well their sound, the Plasmatics' image was innovative, too. It foreshadowed the *Mad Max* style and the whole post-apocalyptic movie genre. Their live performances were true theatrical productions, with TV sets being smashed to pieces, solos consisting of electric guitars being cut by chainsaws, and explosions. On 16 November 1979, during a concert at the Palladium in New York, the band blew up a black Cadillac with dynamite. The following year Wendy W jumped out of a moving Cadillac just before it exploded and catapulted off Pier 62 into the Hudson River. Also in 1980 the umpteenth Cadillac – plunged into a swimming pool this time – was photographed by Swenson for the cover of the first LP.

Rod Swenson: *After getting the record company to approve the budget, getting a late-model Cadillac was no problem since we were scouting for cars like this to blow up in our stage show all the time. The biggest problem was finding a location: no one wanted to have a car driven into their pool for fear of damaging the pool. Of course, I explained that we were planning to use a crane to lower it in carefully but that didn't help; they were still afraid we would crack and wreck their pool. Finally, I thought of my old friend Dr Oliver York, who ran what was then America's biggest nudist park in New Jersey. I had run the restaurant there many years before, and Wendy and I would go there to relax when we had the chance. He trusted me and was always willing to step out over the line and immediately said 'Okay'. So that was where we did it – many of the spectators that day (who you can't see in the photo) all standing around nude watching the photo shoot. It was a great day, we got the shot and everyone was very happy!*

New Hope for the
Wretched
Plasmatics
Stiff America
1980

4FT

Photographer	## Edo Bertoglio
Album	# Welcome Back
Artist	# Plastics
Year	# 1981

This was the second electronic art-pop album by the Plastics, a weird, eccentric band whose brief career met with little acclaim. Misunderstood and underrated at the time, as a Japanese New Wave group they were later to have a big influence on many pop bands such as the Polysics, Pizzicato Five and Stereo Total, who were so inspired by their image and music that they used and covered some of their tracks.

They arrived in the US thanks to the contacts their vocalist, Toshio Nakanishi, had with the Talking Heads, which helped him to enter into a contract with the manager of the B-52's. They became part of the underground scene in New York during the early 1980s.

Their sound is a jerky, frenetic, neo-futurist electro-punk – a mixture of Devo and the B-52's. They borrowed images from 1960s American kitsch culture to accompany caustic, satirical texts inspired by Western consumerism and the then-new craze for technology of the late 1970s.

Welcome Back
Plastics
Invitation
1981

Photographer	**Ebet Roberts**
Album	**Half Alive**
Artist	**Suicide**
Year	**1981**

This album, which came out in 1981, contains tracks of demo tapes and concerts recorded between 1974 and 1979. At the time, the independent label ROIR (Reach Out International Records) was known for issuing innovative material by new American groups on cassette, with catchy graphics and packaging. Even the colour of the plastic cases and the cassettes themselves had an aesthetic value; they were cult objects – symbols of an emerging *avant-garde*.

Later, *Half Alive* would be issued also in vinyl format.

Suicide was a musical project that was the brainchild of the artist and sculptor Alan Vega and the musician Martin Rev. The music and sound were innovative, and the tracks they put together were a sort of proto-industrial synth-punk, with insistent, alienating rhythms. This blazed a trail for many synth-pop and techno groups in the years that followed.

Alan declaimed stories dealing with love and death, while Martin played an old Farfisa keyboard and synthesizers, accompanied by a drum machine that had a skeletal, minimal sound. To call their performances concerts is limiting: they were veritable happenings, where the aim of the artists was not to elicit applause from the audience but rather to provoke with disturbing actions, and to use poetry to reach listeners who often felt justified in walking out before the encore.

Alan Vega: *When it came to our live shows, we didn't want to entertain people. We wanted to throw the meanness and nastiness of the street right back at the audience. If we sent them all running for the exits, that was considered a good show. Some nights we'd barricade the doors so they had no choice but to stay and listen. Every night was like fighting a revolution.*

Ebet Roberts: *I took the picture on 20 January 1980 and I think it was at Alan's loft in New York, but it might have been Marty's; it was a really interesting place with lots of posters and art. I had photographed them a few days earlier with Ric Ocasek, who was working with them at the Power Station Studio.*

Half Alive
Suicide
ROIR
1981

KODAK SAFETY FILM 5063
Special
99
CIGARETTES
58
→24
→25
→27A
→29
→29A
→30A
→31

→7A   →8   →8A   →10
FILM 5063   KODAK SAFETY FILM 5063   KODAK SAFETY FILM 5063

13A   →14   →14A   →15   →15A   →16   K
KODAK SAFETY FILM 5063   KODAK SAFETY FILM 5063

19A   →20   →20A   4 7 3   →21A
FILM 5063   KODAK SAFETY FILM 5063   KODAK SAFETY FILM

→11   →11A   →12   →12A   →13   →
KODAK SAFETY FILM 5063   KODAK SAFETY FILM 5063

→17   →17A   →18   →18A   →19   →
SAFETY FILM 5063   KODAK SAFETY FILM 5063   KODAK SAFETY

→23   →23A   →24   →24A   →25   →2
KODAK SAFETY FILM 5063   KODAK SAFETY FILM 5063

Photographer	**Esther Friedman**
Album	**Zombie Birdhouse**
Artist	**Iggy Pop**
Year	**1982**

This was Iggy Pop's seventh solo album: sixteen tracks recorded in June 1982 at Blank Tape Studios in New York.

The musicians included Chris Stein on guitar (he was also the producer) and another member of Blondie, Clem Burke, on drums.

The album aroused some controversy among critics. I imagine it can't have been easy for established critics to accept following the huge commercial success of previous albums on the Arista label.

In my view, this album is totally permeated by the singer's exceptional brilliance: there is automatic writing, dissonant free singing, rich creativity and experimentation.

You could call it Iggy's notebook, containing notes that he would probably use in the future. In this sense it is by definition an 'album' – a collection of ideas, sounds, words and images – although, to be honest, I cannot find a connecting thread.

The brilliance of this album is the very lack of an overall concept: the songs follow on one from the other in a sort of surrealist *cadavre exquis* (exquisite corpse).

Zombie Birdhouse
Iggy Pop
Animal Records
1982

New Wave and the first British LPs

Photographer	# Peter "Kodick" Gravelle
Album	## Damned Damned Damned
Artist	## The Damned
Year	## 1977

Damned Damned Damned was the debut album of the punk rock band the Damned. Issued in the UK by the Stiff Records label in 1977, it can be considered a classic of the early punk of the 1970s.

After the success of the single 'New Rose' and following their turbulent tour with the Sex Pistols, the Heartbreakers and the Clash, the band went to the Pathway Studio to record their own album with the record producer Nick Lowe, who had already worked on the recording of 'New Rose'. After ten days' work in the studio, the final mix was completed on 15 January 1977.

Damned Damned Damned was issued in the UK by Stiff Records on 18 February 1977 – the 22nd birthday of the band's guitarist, Brian James – and on 16 April the same year in the US.

The band's ironic approach is expressed in music through banter, humour and grimaces (the last well represented on the cover of this first album). These elements, combined with a very fast musical tempo typical of garage rock, ensured the album's success.

Stiff Records 'deliberately' pressed the first copies of the album with, on the back of the cover, a photograph of the band Eddie and the Hot Rods instead of the Damned, subsequently placing a sticker on the cover explaining the printing error – thus arousing the interest of collectors and enthusiasts and boosting the album's sales. The design is credited to Big Jobs Inc., the pseudonym of Barney Bubbles.

Peter Gravelle: *I don't know where I came up with the pie idea. It was my idea. I think it was just because I thought it would be visually effective. On the day of the shoot Judy and Patti were the stylists and in charge of picking up custard or cream pies. We all arrived at the studio and there were no cream pies to be found. They had picked up some flan bases, shaving cream and ketchup and mustard. Well, that would have to do... I have to say, the boys were very cool about the whole thing – mentholated shaving cream does sting the eyes. Yes, I was in control. Someone has to be. It was my photo shoot. Looking back, it was a case of random bits all coming together with no real meaning to begin with. Don't think about it, just do it...*

Damned Damned Damned
The Damned
Stiff Records
1977

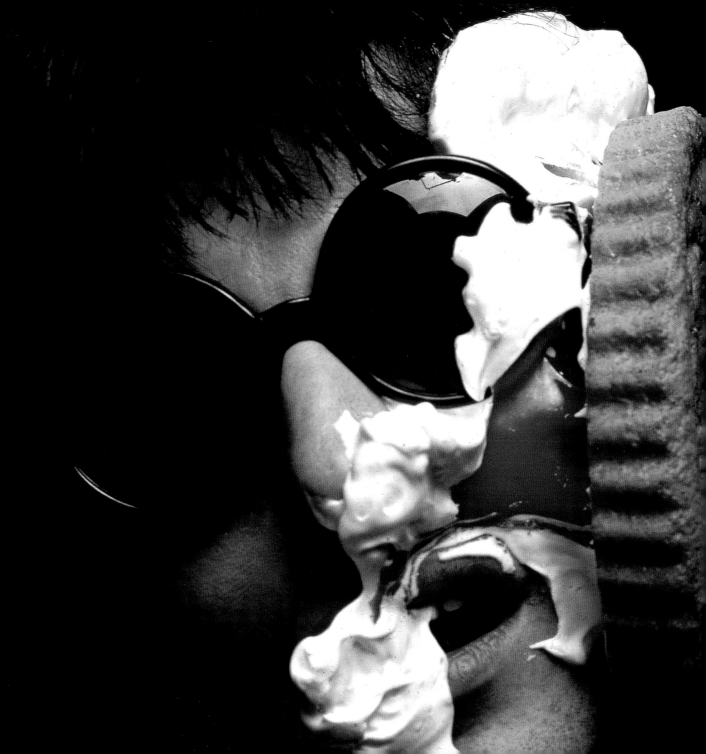

Despite his habit of buying second-hand clothes, for his debut album released on the Stiff Records label on 30 September 1977, Ian Dury bought new shoes and trousers.

The disc is considered one of the first classic punk albums released in the UK, even though the lyrics of Dury's songs often avoid the anti-establishment stance associated with the movement in 1977. Indeed, Dury preferred to sing love songs or tell stories of working-class characters set in London's East End or Essex, where he grew up. These songs are often vulgar and bawdy, but filled with humour and affection for his characters. Ian Dury also stood apart musically, using different styles that reflected his background – alternating disco tracks with pub rock, funk and an early rock 'n' roll sound.

The album photo was shot by Chris Gabrin outside a lingerie shop at 306 Vauxhall Bridge Road, Westminster, close to Victoria Station.

Ian Dury appears with his five-year-old son, Baxter, and the picture was apparently the result of chance. As the singer often recounted, his son suddenly appeared on set, and thus that moment – which looks contrived and posed – was immortalized.

Chris Gabrin: *I only shot 24 exposures and Baxter was in just 4 of them. As soon as the films were developed, Ian came round and we immediately chose the same shot. We were so excited by the picture that we went straight into my darkroom and made the first print. The album title* New Boots and Panties!! *was subsequently coined by Ian.*

New Boots and Panties!!
Ian Dury
Stiff Records
1977

Martyn Goddard

In the City

The Jam

1977

Martyn Goddard: *I had a phone call from Bill Smith, one of the art directors at Polydor Records, in late February 1977. He had to produce an LP cover for a new band, which he was excited about, but, as usual, it was an urgent assignment as the record company wanted to release the album in May. The New Wave band was named The Jam, a three-piece outfit comprising of Bruce Foxton, Rick Buckler and Paul Weller, who, to quote Bill, 'is a bloke with definite ideas about the group's image'. At this point I hadn't met any member of the band or seen a photograph. Bill's concept for the cover was to photograph the group in an urban location featuring a wall of white tiles with a graffiti-sprayed logo, as the album title was* In the City. *I thought of all the problems a location shoot would incur because of the need to spray paint on a wall and the permissions and permits that would be required. It was decided to shoot in my studio in Kensington Church Street using a couple of 8- x 4-in [20- x 10-cm] flats tiled in 4-in [10-cm] white Crystal tiles. I can't remember whether it was budget or time constraints but Bill and I tiled the flats the morning of the session, 2 March 1977, and it was Bill who took the black spray paint and in one attempt produced the iconic logo on the white ceramic tiles as the glue was setting.*

The band arrived at my cramped studio wearing mod suits and carrying Rickenbacker guitars. Bruce's bass was a copy at this time and Rick brought a snare drum. I have since learned that the band had to scramble the clothes together in the mad rush to release the record, and the old trainers worn that day were replaced in later shoots by two-toned leather loafers. We didn't hang around; after the hairdresser had trimmed their hair, we were all ready to shoot. Looking at my original photo journal, I used two large studio flashlights with metal reflectors either side and close to the lens of my Hasselblad 500C/M camera to produce a fashion-style shadowless effect. I shot Polaroid test prints, which only needed minor adjustments before clipping a black-and-white film back on the camera and shooting two rolls of film that were to become the front cover. Bill and I then set about photographing the wall in various stages of distress, Bill smashing tiles and spraying new words. I photographed the vandalism of the wall of tiles, which were used as the back cover.

In the City
The Jam
Polydor
1977

55

56

63

Photographer	**Gered Mankowitz**
Album	**Ultravox!**
Artist	**Ultravox!**
Year	**1977**

A contract with the Island label was offered to a very young Steve Lillywhite (later known as producer of the Simple Minds and U2, to name the most famous) and signed with the new name: Ultravox!

Warren Cann: *The name Ultravox! sounds like an electronic device, so it represents the band's essence really well.*

February 1977 saw the release of the single 'Dangerous Rhythm/My Sex', which earned the best reviews of the band's career. Brian Eno had a hand in its production, and he made it one of the greatest debut singles, along with the Sex Pistols' 'Anarchy in the UK'. It was immediately followed by an album, in which the track 'My Sex' was Eno's most direct contribution.

Billy Currie: *'My Sex' was one of those tracks that write themselves. Eno really liked the lyrics, written by John Foxx. I improvised some chords on the piano. Eno brought his Minimoog into the studio and showed me some sounds, which I then used also on 'Slip Away'.*

At the time, synthesizers were out of fashion. Until David Bowie's album *Low* was released, electronic music had been considered incongruous, being too close to Pink Floyd, which punk musicians detested. The fanzine *Sniffin' Glue* described the album as 'electronic punk music – a cross between the Doctors of Madness and Roxy Music'. 'My Sex' is a wonderful song, with its ghostly, oppressive, languid atmosphere and with a powerful emotional impact drawn from Foxx's own personal experience. The lyrics were influenced by J G Ballard, and place the writer at the heart of this new style of urban music.

Gered Mankowitz: *The Ultravox! cover was shot around the Island Records studio and was a pretty dynamic shoot because of John Foxx's energy, vision and creativity – he was inspiring to work with and I was delighted to have had the opportunity.*

Ultravox!
Ultravox!
Island Records
1977

Masayoshi Sukita

Heroes

David Bowie

1977

Towards the end of 1977 the RCA record company launched an advertising campaign under the slogan: 'There's Old Wave. There's New Wave. And there's David Bowie.' Nothing could have been more spot-on for Bowie's latest album – from a musician who throughout his career had always successfully absorbed youth culture and youth trends through the prism of his own unique, personal vision.

Although some bands and managers merely exploited the punk movement to create spinoff commercial products, artists such as Bowie acted as catalysts for its aesthetic, which could thus bring about a rich cultural exchange – as Bowie had with Iggy Pop at the time.

Bowie's *Heroes* and Iggy Pop's *The Idiot* are twin brothers who compare themselves with each other and swap ideas, musicians and images of their everyday life in Berlin.

These are the signs – and not only musical ones – that bear total witness to the cultural ferment that was taking place in 1977.

Masayoshi Sukita: *In 1977 when David Bowie produced Iggy Pop's album, they came to Japan together for promotion of the album. I just wanted to shoot portraits of both of them – not for an album cover or any other media uses, but just for my work. So I asked them and they gave me the okay; I could have a one-hour photo session with each.*

The only thing Bowie asked me was to prepare some leather jackets. I didn't ask him to do anything special – I believe that it's best to shoot depending on each individual situation. I was just concentrating on capturing good moments in his unique movements.

A month or so later, I chose about 15 shots and sent them to Bowie. He asked me if he could use the image for the cover of an upcoming album. I learnt from the session how important it was to make my brain blank and believe in my own senses.

Heroes
David Bowie
RCA Victor
1977

Photographer	**Chris Gabrin**
Album	**This Year's Model**
Artist	**Elvis Costello**
Year	**1978**

This is Elvis Costello's second album, recorded chiefly at Eden Studios in west London with the band the Attractions.

Early versions of the album have a cover that looks poorly printed, which cuts off the left-hand edge of the image (between the E of 'Elvis' and the T of 'This') and reveals the printer's colour bar on the right-hand side. This was another deliberate mistake on the part of Barney Bubbles.

The US version of the album has another photograph from the same session.

Chris Gabrin: *The concept of him behind a camera for the sleeve of* This Year's Model *had already been chosen, so I decided to equip Elvis with exactly the same tripod and camera as I was using, to create a 'mirror' for him. Alongside a powerful stereo, I kept a large record collection at my Camden studio, and artists would choose music they enjoyed or were interested in for their sessions. Just as we were about to start shooting, Elvis asked me if I had* Hotel California *by the Eagles, and could I play it? I was puzzled by his choice – until he told me that he loathed the record, but wanted to look really pissed off and angry in the shots! We played the record several times during the session and, while I directed him, I was also aware of his copying some of my own actions as I took the photographs.*

This Year's Model
Elvis Costello
Radar Records
1978

N963 B

Photographer	**Keith Collie**
Album	**Stateless**
Artist	**Lene Lovich**
Year	**1978**

The daughter of a Serbian father and an English mother, Lene Lovich (real name Lili-Marlene Premilovich) was born in Detroit. When she was almost 13 she moved to Europe, where she gained broad work experience – as a mime, recording screams for horror movies and as a writer for the French disco star Cerrone. In London she went to art school, where she met the guitarist Les Chappell. In 1974 the pair formed the funky soul group the Diversions, and recorded a couple of singles. In late 1977 Lene Lovich joined the Oval Exiles, and recorded a demo tape with them on which she played saxophone and sang backing vocals. She sang solo only on 'I Think We're Alone Now', a cover of the famous hit by Tommy James & the Shondells. The track caught the eye of Dave Robinson at Stiff Records, who decided to offer her a contract. The year 1978 saw the release of the album *Stateless*, which was somewhat thrown together but nevertheless pleasant, and was interesting for its peculiar vocal style, full of warbles and Slavic sonorities. Her appearance, too, was rather original – a curious fusion of past and present, like the styles and musical genres that went into her music. Lene wore her hair in long plaits, and had ample skirts, veils, shawls and old-fashioned earrings, all of which contributed to giving her the image of a woman closely tied to her cultural distinguishing marks, with a strong identity – a cross between a gypsy woman and a traditional witch.

Lene Lovich: *The outfit is an actual piece of old clothing – a cheap way of getting a unique item. I really like '40s shapes: strong, geometric. The '80s copies of shoulder pads didn't look quite right when you compared them with the '40s.*

Stateless
Lene Lovich
Stiff Records
1978

Photographer	**Brian Griffin**
Album	**Stateless**
Artist	**Lene Lovich**
Year	**1978**

Griffin photographed Lene Lovich for the second pressing of the album in a singular stage outfit. The singer, wearing a grey suit with a military cut, is immortalized in robotic poses and syncopated movements. It is a portrait of the heroine of a totalitarian, sci-fi future that inevitably brings to mind Fritz Lang's film *Metropolis* or George Orwell's novel *Nineteen Eighty-Four*.

Brian Griffin: *I was influenced by German image-making of the '30s.*

It was shot in a rehearsal studio in Pentonville, London, using an Olympus OM1 35mm camera.

Stateless
Lene Lovich
Stiff Records
1978

Gered Mankowitz

Generation X

Generation X

1978

Generation X were active from the very start of the UK punk movement. In 1976 they were already well known on the London scene. Before calling themselves Generation X, they performed under the name Chelsea, with the singer Gene October.

It's clear that the band always gave a nod in the direction of pop, both musically and in the image seen here. Although their punk rock is spare, hard and electric, it contains sophisticated, sometimes harmonious sounds, finished off with an excess of effects. The same polish can be seen in the appearance of each member of the band. Clearly nothing has been left to chance, from the threadbare T-shirt to the carefully tousled hair – all details that give them the look of a fashion band and make them more commercial than the rest.

After the band broke up, each member of Generation X continued their own musical career, entering showbiz in a big way.

Billy Idol stands out from the rest – he was a pop star in every sense from the early 1980s onwards. The other members were to join very well-known bands including Sigue Sigue Sputnik, the Sisters of Mercy, Carbon/Silicon, Gene Loves Jezebel, The Cult and The Alarm.

Gered Mankowitz: *Billy Idol walked into my studio and asked me to do for the band what I had done for the Stones back in the '60s. I was pretty blown away as nobody had referenced my earlier work like that before and it felt flattering but also a bit intimidating! They were a very visual band though and got into the session with enthusiasm and energy, and I think the portraits were successful and have stood the test of time.*

Generation X
Generation X
Chrysalis
1978

Jim Rakete:

The Promise

I remember that lengthy loft in Berlin's Kreuzberg that I had just rented, full of daylight. Not yet my new studio, not yet filled with any equipment or lights, smelling of fresh paint. I remember facing that white wall that was sticking out of the grey concrete floor like an innocent piece of paper out of a typewriter, waiting for a first sentence.

And I remember Nina Hagen that Sunday morning, bringing her boyfriend/bassist Manne, a Rickenbacker guitar and a large mirror that she had spray-painted 'Nina Hagen Band' on to that first shooting. Her innocent face with these huge eyes that could change from innocent curiosity to a hard stare in a heartbeat. Her pale complexion made up like an opened paint box, her body in a tight black catsuit, her electrified hairstyle.

Anyone with a sense of brain would have taken these pictures in colour, given the crazy shade-tones of her make-up, but, strangely enough, we used good, old Tri-X in black and white.

We were well aware we were writing that first sentence of a story both of us underestimated at the time. We were stating something. What?

For some reason I watercoloured some of the prints later, just using different shades of indigo and skintone Schmincke colour – a demo at best; I believed I'd be able to redo those properly in the weeks to follow. But we never did. Given the time pressure of the pre-release of the album in West Berlin, it was decided to use that demo as a record cover and tour poster.

When we had ended that shooting day with Nina, I could feel six 35mm films in my right jeans pocket – the majority of the shots taken outside by the canal, and on some field at the outskirts of town. But of all these, it was the one no-nonsense picture of Nina with the cigarette – she didn't even smoke – that signed, sealed and delivered Nina's statement. A photographical portrait is two people looking for a secret with a camera, ending with an image that can be a promise. It can last a long time, if that promise is kept.

Nina Hagen Band
Nina Hagen Band
Epic
1978

Photographer **Gered Mankowitz**

Album Reality Effect

Artist The Tourists

Year 1979

The Tourists' second album met with more success than their first, staying in the UK top 100 for 16 weeks. It was to open the door to success for Annie Lennox and her partner, Dave Stewart, the future Eurythmics.

It's a light pop-rock album with little to distinguish it, compared with the discs the Eurythmics were to produce later. What is interesting here is the engaging cover shot by Gered Mankowitz, which immediately references a punk aesthetic – demonstrating that by 1979 a massive commercial exploitation of punk stereotypes was under way. The snow-white, ghostly interior is splattered with Jackson Pollock-like paint, the purity of Annie Lennox in a wedding dress besmirched with splashes of colour. This 'violent' work is impeccably punk – from a visual rather than a musical point of view. *Reality Effect* is an album more for looking at than for listening to.

Gered Mankowitz: Reality Effect *was shot on a set we built in my studio after long discussions with Annie and Dave. The idea was that the band would begin to colour the pure white room in a natural and realistic way using the non-toxic children's paints that I supplied – it was supposed to be a 'painting by numbers' exercise. However, unknown to me, a couple of the band had dropped acid beforehand and as we begun the shoot the drug kicked in and all discipline went out of the window, as the paint was hurled everywhere and we ended up with the amazing result, which was much more exciting than we had visualized!*

Reality Effect
The Tourists
Logo
1979

Photographer	**Martyn Goddard**
Album	**Three Imaginary Boys**
Artist	**The Cure**
Year	**1979**

I am the vacuum cleaner, Robert is the lamp and Michael is the fridge.
– Laurence Andrew 'Lol' Tolhurst

An excellent album by the three members of the Cure. The songs are musically sparse and simple, the lyrics marked by writing that is bitter, unstructured and extremely punk. Just three lads playing in a room (the room on the cover, perhaps?). Many of the lyrics are nonsense – their sole function being to sustain the music. The cover picture plays a crucial role, representing the band's 'non-image'. This, together with the music, conveys that existential angst and inability to relate to the real world, that spleen that was to stay with the band throughout their career, that dark poetry that later would spawn a veritable youth movement.

Three Imaginary Boys
The Cure
Fiction Records
1979

Photographer **Masayoshi Sukita**

Album **Solid State Survivor**

Artist **Yellow Magic Orchestra**

Year **1979**

Yellow Magic Orchestra was a musical project put together by Haruomi Hosono (bass, keyboards, vocals), Yukihiro Takahashi (drums, vocals), Ryuichi Sakamoto (keyboards, vocals) and the digital programmer Hideki Matsutake.

Its members were interested in experimenting and made use of new electronic equipment. Already as early as 1970 Matsutake had developed, with the electronic musician Isao Tomita, composition methods and techniques that would later be used and put into practice by Yellow Magic Orchestra.

To make *Solid State Survivor*, born of the idea of making a fusion between exotic Orientalism and modern electronic music, the group used IT, synthesizers and electronic percussion.

The cover picture of the musicians, who look like dummies, automata or machines, helps to convey the idea of the synthetic – a recurring idea among various emerging New Wave musicians. YMO were often seen as influential innovators in the field of electronic music, and they contributed to the development of synth-pop, ambient house, electronica, electro and other genres.

Masayoshi Sukita: *I had been chosen for the photo session for* Solid State Survivor. *At the time, I was into a Chinese game, mah-jong, so I owned a table for mah-jong. When I saw the table, I got an idea to use it for the SSS session. Mah-jong needs four people to play, and the band had only three members – that's why I added one of the mannequins.*

The image has two versions of background colours, green and purple. The green version was used for the album cover.

Solid State Survivor
Yellow Magic Orchestra
Alfa Records, Inc.
1979

Photographer	**Masayoshi Sukita**
Album	**真空パック (Vacuum Pack)**
Artist	**Sheena & The Rokkets**
Year	**1979**

We've always been a 100 per cent punk band in terms of attitude.
– Makoto Ayukawa

Before joining the band I was what you might call a 'kitchen singer', but it was Patti Smith who really taught me to sing.
– Etsuko Ayukawa (Sheena)

One of the most famous bands on the Japanese mentai rock scene, Sheena & The Rokkets formed in 1978. Their singer, Etsuko Ayukawa, used the pseudonym Sheena in tribute to the Ramones. They were Elvis Costello's backing band during his Japanese tour.

On this second album, produced by Haruomi Hosono of Yellow Magic Orchestra, the group's sparse rock 'n' roll clashes with the sonority of the producer's synthesizer, creating an interesting interaction.

Makoto Ayukawa: *Music should have a big jacket, played on a turntable, not something convenient like MP3s. A record is a living thing. You have to take care of it; you can't go out of the room and leave it because you have to be ready to lift the needle up.*

Masayoshi Sukita: *I didn't have specific ideas for the photo session of this. I went into a supermarket on the way to the photo studio for the session, where I accidentally found wrapping cellophane. I hit on an idea to use it for the session like that.*

真空パック (Vacuum Pack)
Sheena & The Rokkets
Alfa Records, Inc.
1979

Photographer	**Brian Griffin**
Album	**Flex**
Artist	**Lene Lovich**
Year	**1979**

I'm quite happy for people to read many different stories into my music. It always interests me when people come up and say, 'I know what that song is about' and they tell me a new story that I haven't ever heard of before. I feel very strongly in people exercising their own imaginations.
— Lene Lovich

Just as Lene Lovich's wardrobe was filled with an eclectic mixture of elements that created a unique, inimitable image, the sounds of her records mix atmospheres and fuse music and musicians from different cultures, producing songs and melodies that are highly personal.

The second album was less successful commercially than the first. However, it was more sophisticated and polished. It was recorded at Wisseloord Studios in Hilversum, Netherlands, using more advanced technology.

Flex is Lene Lovich's most introverted album. Its songs deal with subjects often inspired by dreamlike images that capture the listener with more powerful emotional force than the debut album did. The texts are kaleidoscopic, lending themselves to many possible interpretations.

The cover shows Lovich playing with some ice hockey pucks inside a stainless-steel fermentation tank in the Guinness brewery at Park Royal, London.

When the album was released it created controversy, and in the US some members of the Baptist Church sought to have its release prohibited, claiming that it depicted an act of witchcraft.

Flex
Lene Lovich
Stiff Records
1979

Photographer	# Tony McGee
Album	## Second Edition
Artist	## Public Image Ltd
Year	## 1979

This is the reissue of *Metal Box*, released on 23 November 1979. Originally, this was released as three 30-cm (12-in) singles in a circular metal container, like those used to hold reels of movie film, but in this second edition it came out with the usual double LP sleeve.

It is a more sophisticated and focused work than the group's debut album. The sonorities and surreal dimension this album creates in the listener's mind are inescapable – a sort of ghostly soundtrack that evokes vivid, magical images, like the cover photograph. Keith Levene described his guitar parts as the process of the disintegration of sound: 'The sound engineers found it really difficult to follow our instructions. Getting such a deep sound out of the bass meant breaking every rule in the book. When I played a chord on the guitar, on the editing machine it must have sounded like the noise of a pane of glass shattering. My guitar was in constant feedback – it seemed as if the sound would carry on forever.'

Second Edition
Public Image Ltd
Virgin
1979

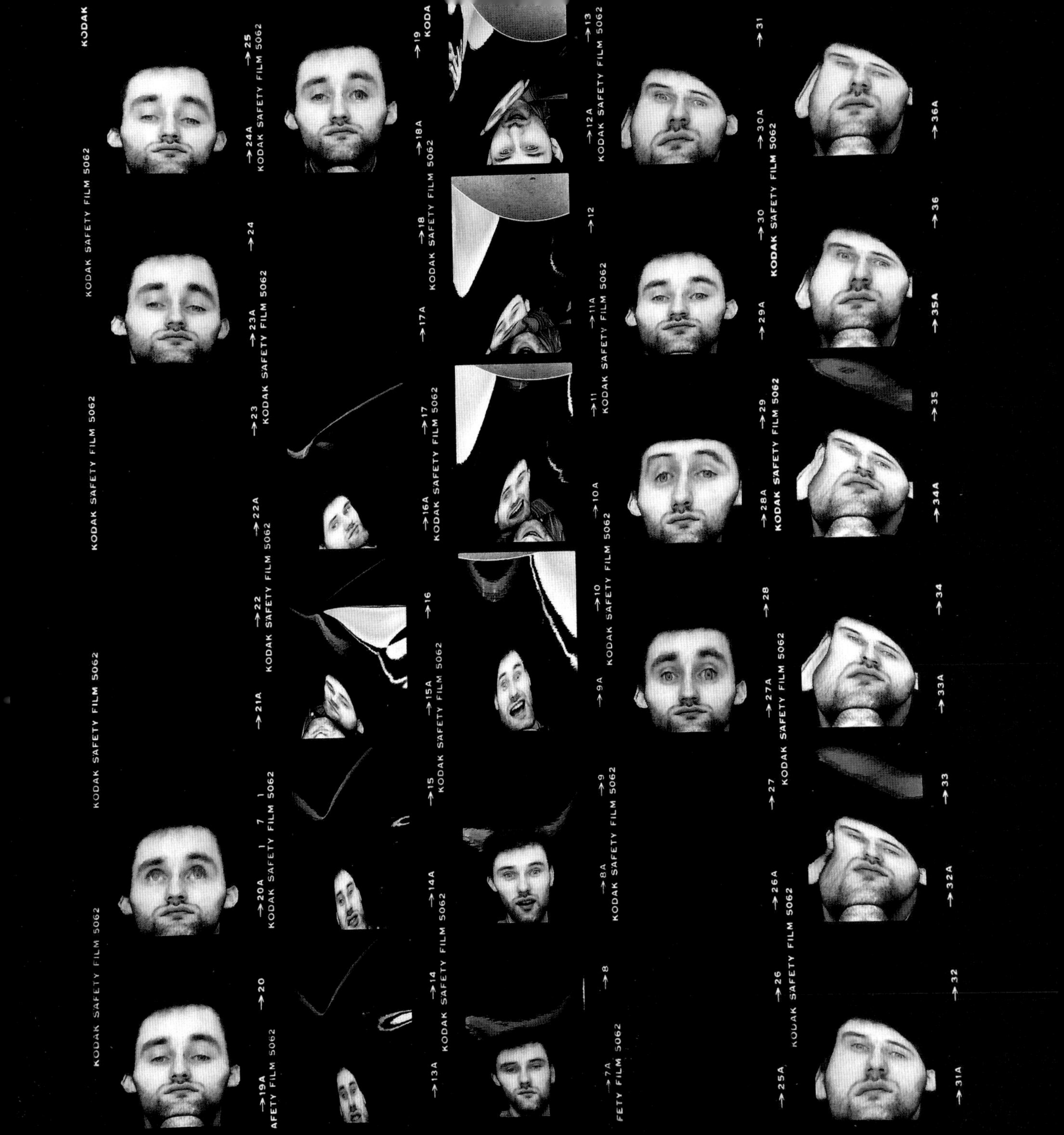
KODAK SAFETY FILM 5062

Photographer	**Alain Bizos**
Album	Unbehagen
Artist	Nina Hagen Band
Year	1979

Unbehagen was the Nina Hagen Band's second album, recorded at Hansa Tonstudio, Berlin, in October and November 1979.

Alain Bizos: *At the end of October 1979, Nina Hagen was recording in a studio near the Berlin Wall; we were on the West side, in a capitalist 'island' in 'communist' East Germany.*

I had just joined the team of the new monthly founded by Jean-François Bizot, and we decided to do a piece on this new German singer.

We arrived in Berlin with the young journalist Elisabetta D. There was instant warmth when we met with Nina – there was good energy, and we were to spend a week together, laughing a lot, listening to her and recording her, completely captivated by her talent. There wasn't a proper shoot. Nina was really at ease with me. We didn't take it too seriously – everything was very spontaneous...

The image CBS would choose for the album Unbehagen *was shot in the street outside the building housing the studio. It was late afternoon, and I deliberately underexposed the sky and the urban landscape, while lighting up Nina with flash. On her head she wore a gold coronet with a blue bird, with which we'd had fun earlier in the day, shooting a series of 'faces' that would become the three famous covers of the second issue of* Actuel *in November 1979... When CBS saw my images in* Actuel *it bought them for several album covers. I don't know why CBS's graphic designer erased the coronet. What a pity!*

Unbehagen
Nina Hagen Band
CBS
1979

Photographer	**Chalkie Davies**
Album	**Specials**
Artist	**The Specials**
Year	**1979**

Music gets political when there are new ideas in music... punk was innovative, so was ska, and that was why bands such as the Specials and the Clash could be political.
    – Jerry Dammers

This was an extremely lucky emerging band, who with this, their first album, produced by Elvis Costello, met with great success in the UK. The album reached number four in the UK charts, and was followed by the single 'Too Much Too Young', which actually got to number one.

    Their music was a combination of ska and an energetic 1960s rocksteady. Its markedly fast rhythms, the competent execution of the reggae and, above all, the focus on political and social themes marked out a distinct punk attitude that set them apart from other emerging ska groups. It should be remembered that in 1979 ska and the mod revival exploded in the UK, leading to a vast production of albums and the arrival of many new bands. It took over the record and film industries, and was relentlessly publicized in the music press. This was the first symptom of the commercial explosion of New Wave, which spawned a huge business that fed on itself, producing hundreds of by-products during the 1980s – new bands, ideas and fashion tendencies, which were created by revisiting and recycling the musical protagonists of the 'New Wave' in 1977.

Specials
The Specials
2 Tone Records
1979

Photographer	**Brian Griffin**
Album	**Look Sharp!**
Artist	**Joe Jackson**
Year	**1979**

This album is a truly explosive mix, triggered by the furious rhythm and extraordinarily multifaceted sound. This is a neurotic and vaguely 'vintage' pop-rock that ranges from sudden bursts of pub rock and irresistible Jamaican vibrations, salsa and reggae and ska to crazy shards of punk'n'roll and jazzy inflections.

Jackson was a great talent, with his soft, gruff singing, his bitter exuberance and the typically British humour of the lyrics, which are acute and sharp – just like the album's title. They alternate between romantic, melancholy love songs and perceptive, caustic observations on typically British social issues, inspired by the Kinks.

The cover photograph is British too: a nice pair of white Denson shoes, immortalized by Brian Griffin. 'It wasn't meant to be on the cover, but when we saw the prints, everyone liked the idea. The artistic director, Michael Ross, borrowed them, and I never saw them again,' Joe Jackson said later.

It isn't an easily accessible album, and a couple of months passed before the public began to appreciate it. But after that, it was a triumph: *Look Sharp!* reached the top 40 in the UK and top 20 in the US. It became a gold disc, and was nominated for the Grammy Awards.

Brian Griffin: *I'd met Joe at the Wimpy in Waterloo Station and we walked to the Hayward Gallery. It was a sunny day and the light was peeping through the crevices. Joe was wearing white Denson winklepickers and a chalk-stripe suit. I just said to him, 'Joe, can you stand there', pointed the camera to the ground and I had the cover...*

Look Sharp!
Joe Jackson
A&M Records
1979

Photographer	**Brian Duffy**
Album	**Lodger**
Artist	**David Bowie**
Year	**1979**

Released by RCA Records in 1979, this album was the last of the so-called 'Berlin trilogy' that also included *Low* and *Heroes*.

It is less introspective than the two preceding albums, and was initially greeted with a certain indifference by critics. Dealing with lighter subjects and containing easier melodies, *Lodger* today is acknowledged to be one of Bowie's most underrated works.

The cover was the result of collaboration between Bowie, the art director, Derek Boshier (a British pop artist), and the photographer Brian Duffy (a well-known fashion photographer, who also shot the images for *Aladdin Sane*).

A low-resolution picture shot with a Polaroid SX-70 camera was deliberately used to produce the grainy effect.

In the album's original gatefold, the photograph of Bowie as a road accident victim appeared with a picture of Che Guevara's corpse and Mantegna's painting *Lamentation Over the Dead Christ*.

Derek Boshier: *The cover for* Lodger *was a collaboration between David, the photographer Duffy and myself. I loved this solution to the problem of David being photographed falling: shooting him from above, on a specially made table built to match the falling form. The table was designed to be completely obscured by David's body. The wash-hand basin was laid underneath the table on the floor.*

Lodger
David Bowie
RCA
1979

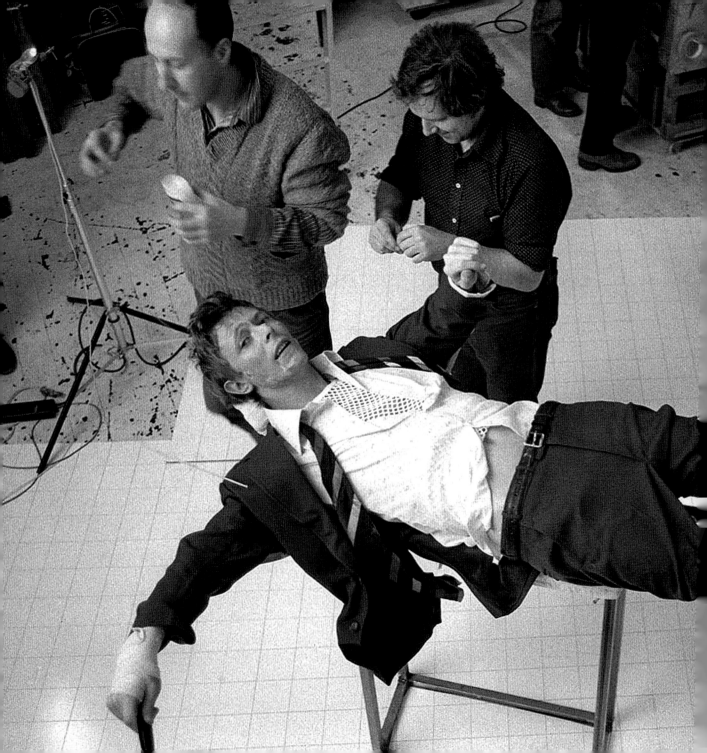

Photographer

Album

Artist

Year

Chalkie Davies
Pretenders
The Pretenders
1980

This album immediately shot up to number one in the UK charts, thanks to masterly production and a playlist that was particularly varied in its rhythms and styles. It should be seen as an important connecting link between the punk culture of the early years and the pop music that was to develop in succeeding years.

The album's success was helped by the presence of Chrissie Hynde, who made her mark as a singer thanks to her strong personality and a certain erotic self-assurance, which set her apart from other emerging singers and offered the band a unique and musically original image.

Chalkie Davies: *I had known Chrissie since her days on the NME and so when the time came for the Pretenders to release their first LP she asked me to take the pictures. Having your photograph taken is one of the unfortunate chores that comes with being in a band. Musicians were concerned with music, not image, but the Pretenders needed an image for their sleeve, not just a photograph. Also it was decided to enforce that image by shooting on a white background so that the band was all you saw – no sets or arty photography.*

That may sound fairly simple, it certainly looks like that when you see the sleeve – just four people on white; that's easy, right? No, it's far from easy, as this was in the days before retouching, before Photoshop allowed us to take a head from here, a body from there, take out some excess flesh, soften the life lines on the face, change the colour of a jacket and pretty much anything you may want. But do that at your peril, for all is well and good until the band shows up on TV and then the myth is blown.

The album sleeve was done in an afternoon. Three changes of clothing were tried, about a dozen rolls of film were taken, but, in the end, only one photo lent itself to being the front cover. You need to get all four personalities to shine through, get four people to look good simultaneously, get four people to project themselves – and only then do you have something good enough to pass the test of time and still be an iconic sleeve decades later.

Pretenders
The Pretenders
Real Records
1980

Photographer	# Brian Griffin
Album	# Crocodiles
Artist	# Echo and the Bunnymen
Year	# 1980

Crocodiles was released on 18 July 1980; it had been recorded in just three weeks at Eden Studios in London and Rockfield Studios, near Monmouth.

The post-punk era was in full swing. You can see it and hear it – the album cover and the music reflect a dark, melancholy inner world.

The lyrics are dreamlike, rich in naturalism and sensuality, alternating with themes of pain and horror – wonderful dreams and subtly terrifying nightmares imbued with a constant sense of mystery. It is a continual interplay between human fears: isolation, death, emotional failure, emotional paralysis, obsession… these were the words most often used to describe this album by the big names in the music press.

And all this is perfectly conveyed in the cover photo, shot by Brian Griffin at night in a wood near Rickmansworth, Hertfordshire.

Originally, the band wanted to include some wooden stakes – an allusion to being burned at the stake – in the background, but eventually it was decided to go with just the studio lights. Apparently, the idea of the stakes was dropped because it might call to mind the Ku Klux Klan.

The cover was mocked by a number of music critics, who described it as an image rich in introspection, desperation and mental confusion.

The music journalist Chris Salewicz wrote a careful, pithy description: '… the Bunnymen are placed in poses of histrionic despair in a near-neurotically gothic woodland that evokes memories of elfin glades and fabled Arthurian legends.'

And *Creem* magazine declared: 'The cover art suggests four boys dazed and confused in a drugged dream, a surreal where-are-we landscape. The Bunnymen's images are of loneliness, disconnection, a world gone awry.'

Brian Griffin: *It was shot on farmland in Rickmansworth near London, using artificial lighting powered by a generator.*

Crocodiles
Echo and the Bunnymen
Korova
1980

Photographer	**Chris Gabrin**
Album	**Metamatic**
Artist	**John Foxx**
Year	**1980**

After leaving Ultravox, John Foxx retired to his London studio, where he recorded his first solo work. It was to become a cornerstone of electronic music.

John Foxx: *I had left the band convinced that electronic music was the future. I read a lot of Ballard. I lived alone in Finsbury Park, walked along disused railway lines and cycled to the studio every day, returning at dawn. I saw myself as the Marcel Duchamp of electro-pop. And the result was* Metamatic.

The album deals with Ballard-like themes: road accidents, views seen through shattered windows, city squares, underpasses and urban wasteland.

The lyrics are like little films, frames that capture snatches of architecture and talk about the modern world, the role of technology and the media, and of an urban environment in the throes of constant change.

Metamatic
John Foxx
Virgin
1980

Photographer	**Brian Griffin**
Album	**Vienna**
Artist	**Ultravox**
Year	**1980**

This is Ultravox's fourth album, produced by the well-known German producer Conny Plank and mixed in a studio near Cologne, Germany. Ultravox had a new lineup, and were led by Midge Ure; they had changed rhythm and style, attracting a new kind of audience that was drawn to the emerging new romantics. The album draws on the black-and-white world of the expressionist films of Robert Krasker, evoking the atmosphere of an exhausted and cynical post-World War Two Vienna at the start of the Cold War. The sounds are a mixture of UK New Wave and the syncopated sparseness of German electronic music.

Griffin's photograph, which yet again fully captures the musical atmosphere, and the clever graphics by Glenn Travis, which are pure and punchy, contribute to giving this album a typically early 1980s look.

Brian Griffin: *This was shot in my studio at 121–123 Rotherhithe Street London, SE16. The set was constructed from one roll of 2.7-m [9-ft] wide white photographic background paper.*

Vienna
Ultravox
Chrysalis
1980

Photographer	**Andy Earl**
Album	See Jungle! See Jungle! Go Join Your Gang Yeah, City All Over! Go Ape Crazy!
Artist	Bow Wow Wow
Year	1981

This was the second album from the New Wave band Bow Wow Wow. It came out in the UK in October 1981, but was never released in the US.

The album cover shows the band's members in a contemporary recreation of Édouard Manet's painting *Le déjeuner sur l'herbe*. Their singer, Annabella Lwin, then aged 15, poses nude. The photograph is by Andy Earl, and the project was overseen by the punk movement's provocateur-in-chief, Malcolm McLaren.

The album aroused controversy precisely because of the image on its cover. The singer's mother demanded a Scotland Yard investigation based on allegations of exploitation of a minor for immoral purposes.

McLaren used the same system as he had with the Sex Pistols to put together a new band: bringing together young musicians of dubious musical quality, but associated with the shocking adolescent image of the young Annabella Lwin, who replaced the group's original singer, the still little-known Adam Ant.

Just as the four members of the Sex Pistols modelled the new line of T-shirts and other garments from the Sex shop, so the young members of this freshly formed group wore a new line by Vivienne Westwood. It was a novel look for a hotchpotch of musical experiments: a mixture of dance music, new post-punk sounds, electronic music and African rhythms.

Today, the image Andy Earl shot of Bow Wow Wow is in the archives of the National Portrait Gallery in London.

See Jungle! See Jungle!
Go Join Your Gang Yeah,
City All Over!
Go Ape Crazy!
Bow Wow Wow
RCA
1981

Fin Costello

Tin Drum

Japan

1981

This was Japan's last studio work.

Despite taking its name from Günter Grass's famous novel, *Tin Drum* was the most Orientalist of all their albums.

The direct contact with Ryuichi Sakamoto was certainly the chief source of inspiration for this record, which is a sophisticated tribute to the Far East in every way, from the lyrics to the songs and the totally minimalist musical arrangements, where electronic elements blend with traditional instruments.

Its innovative drive and special quality might suggest a debut album, but paradoxically it is, as stated above, their last work.

It's an intricate collage of exotic and esoteric musical landscapes, put together with impeccable aesthetic sensibility, and has often been labelled as art-rock, where nothing seems to be left to chance. The same message is conveyed by the cover, which encompasses all the musical elements present in the album, skilfully combined with a balance that is never excessive. This ad hoc shot by Fin Costello certainly contributed to raising the profile of this final tour de force by Japan.

Tin Drum
Japan
Virgin
1981

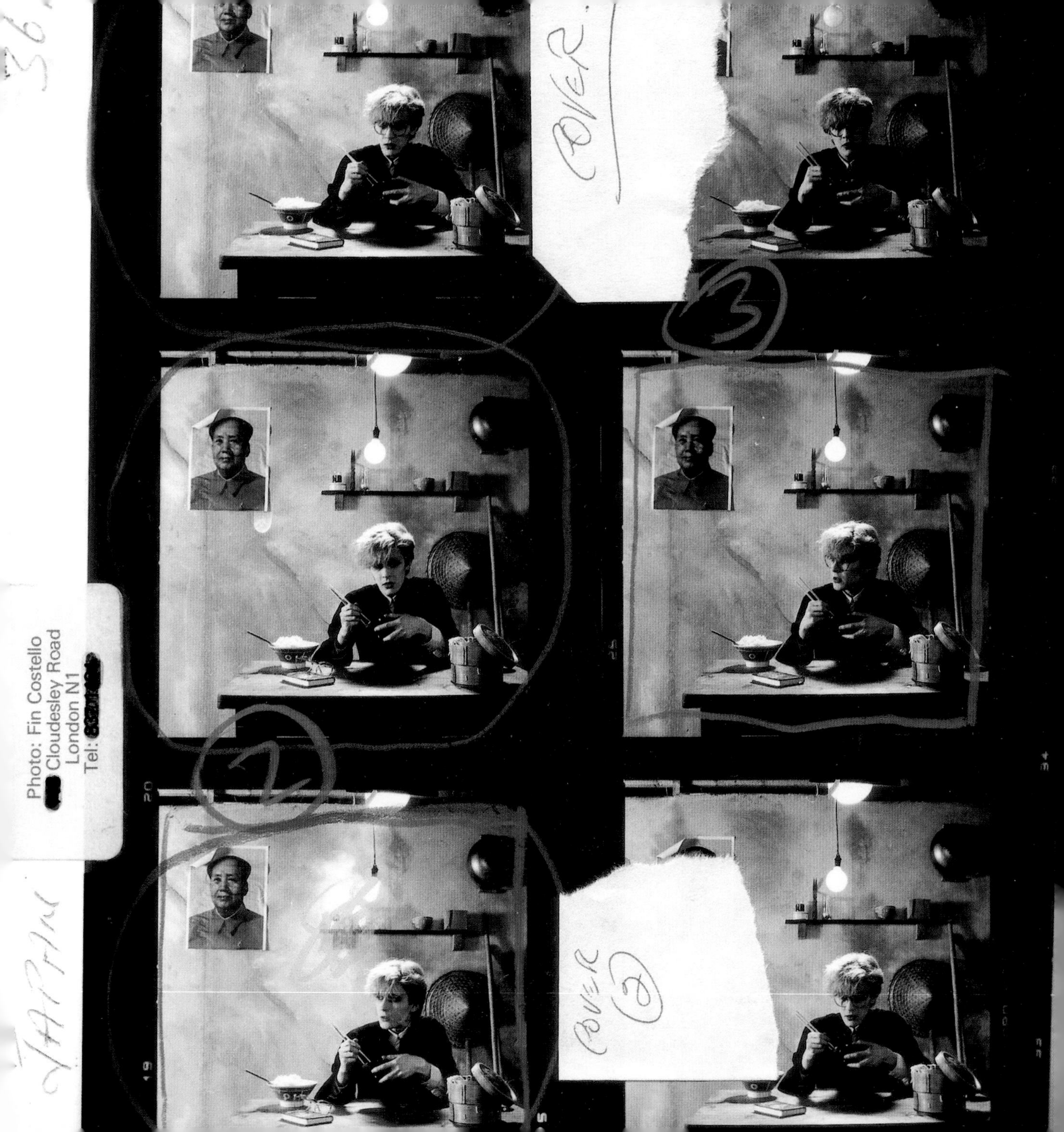

Photographer	# Brian Griffin
Album	# A Broken Frame
Artist	# Depeche Mode
Year	# 1982

Depeche Mode's second album was made in 1982 and was considered by Martin Gore himself to be 'the worst album' in the band's history. That year, synthesizers and drum machines were all the rage – polyphonic synthesizers were being manufactured in large numbers and were inexpensive, and this was a time when music was particularly strongly influenced by technological innovation. The music market was flooded with electro-pop, new romantics and synth-pop. Out of the ashes of New Wave there arose a musical scene in which catchy little songs, and lyrics and music that were often melancholy and introspective, proliferated. These sounds were more commercial and accessible to a mass market. *A Broken Frame* was one among many.

Credit is due for the cover, though, which is a sublime revisiting of Kazimir Malevich's painting *The Reaper on Red*. The peasant woman, wearing clothes by the fashion designer Jacqui Frye, was immortalized by Griffin on a suitably rainy day. The subject, strongly influenced by socialist realism, acquires a dramatic intensity heightened by the sky in the background, which gives the image a touch of German romanticism and made it an icon of 1980s pop.

A Broken Frame
Depeche Mode
Mute
1982

Photographer	**Eugene Merinov**
Album	**Press the Eject and Give Me the Tape**
Artist	**Bauhaus**
Year	**1982**

We present ourselves as honestly as possible. What happens on stage represents all our interests, which range from the writings of Rimbaud, Edgar Allan Poe and William Burroughs to the music of John Cale, Brian Eno, Marc Bolan and David Bowie.
    – Peter Murphy

This album was initially given away for free with the first 30,000 copies of *The Sky's Gone Out*. Later it was issued as a separate record. It contains tracks recorded live in London in 1981 and in Liverpool in 1982. The cover picture was shot by Merinov during a concert in New York in 1981.

From the start, the band felt most at home playing live, where their theatrical performances led to audience participation worthy of the theatre of cruelty, alternating with situations imbued with gothic imagery. In live performance the four members of Bauhaus managed to express themselves with a force verging on the grotesque. *Press the Eject and Give Me the Tape* succeeds in conveying that emotional intensity and dark theatricality to the listener, even without the visual involvement that comes from being in a live audience. The sounds on this record manage to raise the curtain – and on stage Peter Murphy is a dead man acting, a bat, a vampire with a skeletal, spiky body heightened by stark lighting and sharp-edged shadows, as the death of Bela Lugosi is announced...

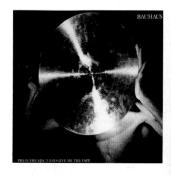

Press the Eject
and Give Me the Tape
Bauhaus
Beggars Banquet
1982

Author **Alberto Lot**

Title # We're Just Heroes, We're Better Than Art

*My poisons are your poisons: love, strength, speed. Do you desire pain, death
or song? Today I bring you a gift brought from the frontiers of consciousness,
a sensation of power that eclipses your new, senseless desires – for be not in
doubt, they are the enemies of order. We will pass unnoticed under the eyes of the
watchmen, disguised as poems.
An added dizziness, the child of frenzy and shadow. Enter, enter. Here
begins the land of the instantaneous; here dwell the miraculously healed
and the convulsionaries. Here, neither the sudden twilight of reawakening nor
reason will be able, despite their lovely white hands, to restrain you.*
– Louis Aragon, *Paris Peasant*, Il Saggiatore, Milan, 1996

Punk was unquestionably the last revolutionary *avant-garde* movement,
not so much in musical terms as for a set of attitudes that unleashed creative
energy almost all over the world. Punk was the teenage child of the historic
avant-garde movements of the 20th century: an unruly, messy child who made few
demands – apart from wanting to change the world. Remember the words on the
shirt from the Westwood-McLaren firm: 'Be Reasonable: Demand The Impossible.'
Much has been written – most of it nonsense. To define it means to kill its true
nature, which is frenzy, desire. The attitude 'I Wanna Be Me' and 'Do It Yourself'
is the very soul of punk, a soul that disowns all parentage, even the most obvious,
out of pure contrariness.

I don't even want to know whether there's been anyone before us in the history books. We want to write a new page, not look back at previous ones. We are a drug. No one can control us.
   – Johnny Rotten

   Punk was a return to street life, loafing about in the mental map of the city seeking new meccas and new myths: myths that lasted the space of a night, of a single record, of a project – sometimes unrealized. This attitude of wandering destructively through spheres of artistic expression produced thousands of records and fanzines, actively involving millions of people in a unique dream that changed the graphic design, fashion and the very language of the world of pop. Fragmentary, inconclusive, speedy and energetic, punk unwittingly created the FUTURE.

   In the movie *Blade Runner*, inspired by *Do Androids Dream of Electric Sheep?* by Philip K Dick, the director Ridley Scott draws heavily on punk imagery: the city inspired by *RanXerox*, the Italian graphic novel series by Tanino Liberatore and Stefano Tamburini, and Gary Numan's 1979 record *Replicas*, which pre-dated the movie by three years and is a sort of sci-fi concept album in which the term 'replicant' is used.

   All this was born of a weariness with the mid-1970s music scene, which had atrophied into rigid forms. The sequins of glam rock had been dissolved by the heroin-addicted sweat of the New York Dolls; progressive rock, with its pompous affectation, had been reduced to a corpse covered in spicy sauces to mask its putrescent state; and packaged, squeaky clean pop had passed away into the ether. Enchanted psychedelic gardens, rock operas, musical extravagances by hippy conservatoire rejects – such grandiosity did not sit well with the angst of anyone who had watched all their hippy illusions destroyed one by one at the hands of power. All this no longer met the needs of a generation in search of a new realism with which to identify. Some preferred to listen to the twisted, urban minimalism of the Velvet Underground; the metallic fury of the Stooges and MC5; the mutant, oblique rock of Brian Eno; or the black masses for harmonium by Nico, the Velvet Underground's angel of death.

   Already, in the 1960s all those who didn't recognize themselves in the culture of peace, love and flower power wound up in New York at that 'court of miracles' frequented by homosexuals, transvestites, drug addicts, lost souls and psychotics that was Andy Warhol's Factory. There, the Velvet Underground found a congenial setting and inspiration. Their music gave those people a voice – a hypnotic, obsessive, diabolical music. Warhol's films, with their unbearable realism, their fixed movie camera trained on those extraordinary beings, became the mirror in which they reflected and transfigured their diversity. These were indiscreet films, probing the dark side. 'I Want to Be a Machine' was Warhol's philosophy – to be just a lens whose glance brushes the surface of things without any ethical or aesthetic intervention – almost a Western version of the Eastern approach of non-action. Except that the Eastern void was replaced by the Western one – the absence of an action filling the space with its vacuousness. Orphans before the lens, these strange beings bared themselves, knowing they would not be judged: the machine doesn't judge – it confines itself to recording. They recreated themselves like stars in a new firmament, in a new Olympus, where their deviancies opened up in all their weirdness, like strange, exotic flowers, displaying their barbaric beauty.

Most of them had no technical training. Therefore, the urgent need to express themselves led them to venture into uncharted waters as amateurs armed only with a love of adventure, in search of pastures new. There was thus a preference for artists practising freer forms of expression, less tied to technical concerns, and at all events artists using more direct and incisive forms of expression, a sort of neo-Dadaism that wanted to get straight to the point rather than get lost in the elaborate convolutions of prog rock or other masturbatory virtuosities. There were many affinities between New Wave and B-movies – an aesthetic based on what is discarded, the poetry of minor stage props, 'we are flowers in the garbage' – against the excessive power of the glossy, well-packaged products promoted by the mass media. Punk wanted to start again from scratch:

Richard Hell: *The intention was to create a real image, like life... it was an anti-glamour, angry aesthetic... there were artists who resembled this. Arthur Rimbaud was like that, as were the characters in François Truffaut's film* Les Quatre Cents Coups [The 400 Blows]. *I remember I had photographs of the film's three protagonists; these were the images that inspired me in 1973. People misunderstood what I wanted to say with* Blank Generation. *For me, blank meant a space that you could fill with whatever you wanted. It was a positive blank, where you could decide to do what you wanted. That's what gave that generation a feeling of power. It meant saying: 'I have rejected all your standards in order to create myself.'*

Lydia Lunch: *New York in the 1970s was a magnificent, ravaged whore – impoverished and neglected after years of abuse. IT STANK OF SEWERS, sex, rotten fish and used diapers. It oozed from everyone's pores. Shit was seeping through already when I was hanging out in Manhattan like a teenage terrorist in '76. I was inspired by the manic ramblings of Lester Bangs in the magazine* Creem, *by the sarcastic intelligence of the Velvet Underground, by the glamour of the New York Dolls' first record and by Patti Smith's poetic improvisation in* Horses. *With 200 bucks in my wallet, stuffed inside a notebook full of long misanthropic wanderings, a baby face that hid the instincts of a prostitute and a murderous urge to create in order to destroy everything that had initially inspired me. I didn't give a flying fuck if the Bowery stank of dogshit. I didn't hang about the toilets of CBGB to write an essay on Duchamp's urinals, but maybe 1977 had a lot in common with 1917 – maybe more than people might have thought at the time. Dada's anti-artistic invasion of Switzerland and the jokes of the surrealists had an explosive energy that pissed on everyone's expectations.*

Michael Belfer: *... we all felt the electricity in the air like a hum from a great transformer that made the air electric with all the possibilities of new art and music that we could come up with.*

Music returned to the streets – we need only look at the pictures of the Ramones, the Heartbreakers, the Jam or Ian Dury. The songs spoke of street life, drugs and prostitution. The image being presented was rough, essential, direct – young hoodlums looking defiant in front of the lens, with the wall of an alleyway in the background. Max's Kansas City, where Warhol's entourage would meet, was a temple to the new metropolitan decadence. Richard Hell flaunting himself, stripped to the waist, with a scornful look, sick with drugs. No time for fine words. I'm ready to be flogged – here's the target. Poetry written in scratches on the skin. Images sharp as a razor blade. Arthur Rimbaud wrote: 'One evening, I sat Beauty on my lap – and I found her bitter – and I insulted her.' Beauty is bitter.

As extreme as Jean Genet, Lydia Lunch was the type of person who would not be afraid to make poetry from her bodily fluids. Desire is always the desire for evil, for brutality. To reconquer power through seduction. Suicide were among the first to reconnect with the lesson of Velvet Underground from the early 1970s, producing extreme performances halfway between Antonin Artaud's theatre of cruelty and the self-harming madness of Iggy Pop when he was with the Stooges. Lydia Lunch described Alan Vega as 'a perverted Puerto Rican, a broken-down Elvis, a psychotic victim of acid'. Suicide performing live were an overwhelming experience.

You could love them or hate them, but you couldn't ignore them. As Roy Trakin wrote: 'They were the first modern rock group to mix music with noise, raising the question of whether noise was music, and vice versa.' Like the early Velvet Underground and the Stooges, Suicide abandoned the song format in favour of performance. Reflecting their artistic background, Suicide built a bridge between the world of art and that of rock, and they were a galvanizing force for the New York underground.

Alan Vega: *We didn't want to entertain people. We wanted to throw the meanness and nastiness of the street right back at the audience. If we sent them all running for the exits, that was considered a good show.*

We are the children of Fritz Lang and Wernher von Braun. We are the link between the 1920s and the 1980s. The impact on society changes completely when there is a pleasurable collaboration with tape recorders, synthesizers and television sets. Our world is an electronic world.
– from the film *Radio On* by Christopher Petit, 1979

Seeking – or fleeing – dangerous ghosts, the Thin White Duke moved to Berlin after playing his role in *The Man Who Fell to Earth*, which had identified him with the alien image of a superman from space. There he found sustenance in the futuristic sounds of krautrock, which drove him to outdo himself once more, moving into colder regions of the soul. Images of swastikas in the mind.

The new lyrics were short. There were fragments of visions, the singing became more detached, the overflowing soul more introverted. And the cutting up of the lyrics only increased their incommunicability. The cut-up technique, discovered by Brion Gysin and famously used in literature by William Burroughs, consisted of taking a text, cutting it into pieces and reassembling it at random, thus creating something new. But cut-up was also derived from the cinematic technique of montage – a modern art *par excellence*. Bowie used the technique as a way of investigating his own past and future. He was himself cut up – for anyone who follows his work comes up against a thousand facets that arise and colour the strange lyrics of his songs, and the changes in the style of his image.

David Bowie: *In my writing I don't necessarily know what I'm talking about; all I do is assemble some things that interest me and use them to create enigmas. This becomes a song, and the people who listen to it take from it whatever they want, whatever they see.*

One of Bowie's plans had been to have Kraftwerk play the opening set at his concerts, but the group needed an enormous amount of equipment, which would have been too expensive for a series of concerts. So Bowie opened his concerts with Kraftwerk's album *Radio-Activity*, played as a soundtrack for a projection of Luis Buñuel's film *Un Chien Andalou*. The image of an eyeball being slit in two, rendered even more bizarre by this musical accompaniment, and its use to open a rock concert, were truly shocking. A futuristic yet nostalgic atmosphere pervaded the venue before the appearance of the Thin White Duke.

On these tours, an idea of austerity predominated – theatricality was conveyed through the sobriety of the set, rather than its lavishness. Bowie used light like painting, flooding the stage with white light of different intensities, creating a chiaroscuro effect delineating different masses. He deliberately chose to dazzle the audience, and the stage displayed an expressionist black-and-white that heightened the hardness of the music and made his image – in black suit and white shirt – stand out as in a cabaret.

The influence of expressionism also appears in the cover photograph of *Heroes* (shot by Masayoshi Sukita), the pose inspired by Erich Heckel's painting *Roquairol*. Almost as if to suggest continuity and common intent between the work of the two artists, the same pose appears in Iggy Pop's album *The Idiot*.

The two albums represent the other side of 1977, a moving on from the punk ideology of *No More Heroes* and a hint at new directions that would lead to post-punk. Music and image tended towards a European aesthetic: angular faces, fixed stares and elegant, decadent expressions with an oblique, philosophical undertone.

The music was crepuscular, and crossed by permanent shards of winter light that swamped all warmth.

A robotic air derived from *Metropolis* can be discerned in Ultravox!'s first record – rigid poses against the background of a squalid urban wall (the poetry of the wall, 'In Berlin by the wall').

John Foxx: *We admired Roxy Music, Steve Harley, David Bowie, Kraftwerk, New York Dolls, Velvet Underground, Iggy Pop and the early Shadows. We loved the futurists, Fritz Lang and film noir; we wanted to build a bridge between German culture and Britain. To develop human involvement with machines – to the point of eroticizing this relationship – has always fascinated me. I believe this started as a child, when I used to watch lots of 1950s films, and also because I grew up in a mechanical and industrial environment in the north of England. There were huge factory complexes, and children played in small areas full of scrapped cars and aircraft, or inside derelict factories. All over the region, roads and motorways had been built almost at random. I remember feeling a mixture of fear and fascination for this new, pitiless environment, when I used to watch cars travelling by night along the filthy motorways.*

Music became filmic. Recovered, lost frames from an imaginary movie projected in the unconscious of a whole generation.

Devo were among the first to re-evoke Kraftwerk's robotic aesthetic, recreating themselves as a 'devolved' army, disciplined and uniform, singing the praises of a world made of plastic and ridiculing rock culture and its myths (as in 'Satisfaction'). In a depersonalized world, there was no longer any room for individualism. The machine was the archetype from which to draw inspiration – it would replace humans, as on the cover of Bill Nelson's *Sound-on-Sound*. And skin would be replaced by plastic ('Your skin is like vinyl'). Recovered, lost frames from an imaginary movie. The filmic quality of the shots of Lene Lovich referenced the imagery of film noir, spy fiction and science fiction, while Nina Hagen posed Liza Minnelli-style on her first album, or as a witch in the morning mist evoked by drug-induced rituals. 'Hey, do you miss me when the nights are long and cold? Do you dream of me in a fog of desire/do you dream of me when I come through the wall like a witch?' she sang in 'Alptraum'.

Voices with a classical/operatic quality sang perverse poems put together along the suburban streets of that decadent, future Berlin that attracted David Bowie and Iggy Pop during those years, and to which Lou Reed devoted his masterpiece *Berlin*. An atmosphere of Mittel-European culture, with its expressionist overtones, returned in the Ultravox album *Vienna*. Klaus Nomi revived the idea of cabaret, blending it with android movements and Japanese kabuki theatre, but this was a return to glam rock and its excesses, which also occurred in the new romantic movement. The new watchword was to invent/become your own hero – not to be a spectator but to be the protagonist of your own imaginary film.

Be a hero – even if for only one day, or one night.

Author # Matteo Torcinovich

Discovery and the Unexpected

Serendipity is looking for a needle in a haystack and finding the farmer's daughter.
  – Julius Comroe Jr, 1976

The images in *Outside the Lines* were born of a search through my vinyl collection.

   The album that kicked off this adventure was the first one made by the Damned, which I like a lot. I bought it in 1977 and it's a special album for me. Its sounds are special. The mixing is unlike other recordings of the time and there are cold sounds which, together, create a flat, grey atmosphere – a sort of neutral hiss. Today, we would call it low-fi. These electronic tribal sounds are extraordinarily unpolished, with rough drum rhythms that force you to listen at a deafeningly high volume. On the back of the cover is the nonsensical instruction: 'Made to be played loud at low volume'. Quite so!

   Aside from all this, I have always found the cover photo of those four damned souls with their smeared faces highly amusing. Extremely punk. Totally British.

Who knows how many photos they shot, how many cakes they splattered into their faces that day… Cakes? Or maybe shaving foam, ketchup or strawberry jam…

So I decided to write to the photographer Peter Kodick. It wasn't hard to find his contact details – googling brings up some 1,300 pages with interesting news and facts about him. He started out as a fashion photographer and was a friend of many punk celebrities of the time. His real name is Peter Gravelle.

I wrote to him, asking whether he had taken other shots of the Damned covered in cream, and whether it might be possible to see them. Despite the naïve tone of my letter, I was astonished to receive very prompt reply:

> *Ciao Matteo,*
> *Nice to hear from you. As regards The Damned record session I shot probably 4 to 5 rolls of 12 exposure with the 4 band members together, then another roll each on individual shots. Is the research you are doing personal or for something particular? Sorry to hear about the terrible rain you are having in Venetcia.*
> *regards, Pete*

We began an exchange of correspondence that was amusing, interesting and rich in intriguing facts. He sent me those unpublished images – and seeing them was like going backstage with the Damned. The alternative, discarded versions give that record and its music a new lease of life.

All this made me so curious that I started looking for the photographers, and the shots, of another 150 records!

I said to myself: if one replied, others will, too. And so it proved.

This research became systematic and focused. I chose photographs for covers that meant something to me, produced between 1976 and 1982.

Alongside this systematic investigation, just as in real life, chance had a hand as well. If a researcher already knew exactly what they were looking for, they wouldn't need to look for it – it would be enough to have confirmation of something they already knew existed.

As well as coming across cases of serendipity, I often found myself in situations where it was impossible to go any farther because, for example, some of the photographers were dead, unavailable or not interested in being cited in a punk context. Some had vanished without trace, like Trevor Rogers. I regret not having been able to contact him and locate alternative pictures for the Stranglers' wonderful *Rattus Norvegicus* (1977).

The same goes for Geoff Howes. And I have therefore been left without much of the photographic material relating to Gary Numan and all the wonderful images of *Replicas* (1979), *The Pleasure Principle* (1979), *Telekon* (1980) and *Assassin* (1982).

However, my worst disappointments were when, although I managed to contact a photographer, I found out that the negatives and contact sheets had been lost.

Every album cover has a story. Those of the most famous ones are well known; other covers hide secrets and yet others simply started out as photographs and then became something special in this context. Often, these led to interesting exchanges between myself and the photographer in question.

A curious case is the cover of Iggy Pop's *The Idiot*. It's an image I've always liked a lot – like the record, which was one of the first that caught my interest. It belongs to what I call the 'Berlin Trilogy': *The Idiot*, David Bowie's *Heroes* and Kraftwerk's *Trans-Europe Express* – records that have many things in common.

No photographer is named among the credits for *The Idiot*. I began to search for who might be responsible by looking through books and magazines. I needed some bit of news, some clue, as a starting point. I continued searching the web, which is always a great resource. The biggest music databases, such as Allmusic and Discogs, attribute the album cover to Andy Kent, as does Wikipedia. At that time, Andy Kent worked a lot with Iggy Pop and David Bowie – he had been their official photographer on tour and he shot the cover of *Lust for Life*. I wrote to him, and Kent replied that someone must have got confused in attributing *The Idiot* to him, for he was not the photographer:

> *Hello Matteo,*
> *I am the photographer for the* Lust for Life *album cover. There was no special shoot for the cover.*
> *It was a BBC studio interview in Birmingham, England. The original negs went to RCA and I was paid extra.*
> *I was his tour photographer. The other negs from the shoot I have!*
> *As to* The Idiot*... I was credited for it... I did not photograph it.*
> *I worked for Iggy and David Bowie in the 70's and someone made a mistake!!*
> *Best regards*
> *Andrew Kent*

Indeed that image, in comparison with that of *Lust for Life*, lacks the American photographer's consummate technique – though the careless focusing and poor quality of the black-and-white print might have been a deliberate choice in order to give the image a punk look.

I knew that Iggy, immortalized in that pose, was playing the role of the character Roquairol in a painting by Erich Heckel. I began to suspect that it might have been Esther Friedman, Iggy's then partner, who took the photo.

I imagined there might be a cultural connection between the painter of *Die Brücke* and Esther, who, as it happened, was German and a photographer. I became convinced the picture was hers.

After about a year I managed to contact Esther Friedman, who kindly let me have some interesting photographs shot for the covers of *TV Eye: Live 1977* and *Zombie Birdhouse*. However, to my question about the photograph on *The Idiot*, she replied with astonishment that she had always thought it was by Kent.

As luck would have it, when Esther and I were writing to each other, David Bowie was in Berlin. Given that they were friends, I asked Esther to consult Bowie, hoping he might have a vague idea who shot the photograph.

Bowie's response was prompt, and so one day I received a letter from Esther:

dear matteo,
mystery solved david bowie took the picture.

That was quite some discovery. I asked Esther to investigate whether there were other shots. Nothing doing. The photograph Bowie shot for *The Idiot* was a one-off Polaroid picture.

The European edition of Kraftwerk's album *Trans-Europe Express* has a lovely 1940s-style retro image. Florian Schneider, Ralf Hütter, Karl Bartos and Wolfgang Flür pose very elegantly before a neutral background of curtains. The static pose recreates the atmosphere of an earlier time, in total contrast with the record's *avant-garde* musical content.

At bottom right is the photographer's delightfully old-fashioned signature: Maurice Seymour. I always thought it was a graphic trick to reinforce the impression of an old photograph, given that it was the custom of photographers in the 1940s and 1950s to sign their work with a logo.

I did some research and discovered that Maurice Seymour was indeed born in 1900, and had owned, with his brother, a photographic studio in Chicago and, later, in New York. He was highly successful, creating portraits of the most fashionable stars of movies and the stage. Maurice Seymour had started out by photographing musicians and actors from the 1930s onwards – and that's why that shot is so perfectly in keeping with that era's style.

I tried to contact Ron Seymour, his son, who did not know Kraftwerk at all. There was nothing among the negatives in the Seymour archive that had any connection to the shoot with that group. Despite this, Ron Seymour recognized his father's signature and style. From this I concluded that, as often happens, the negatives must have been bought by the record label or by the group themselves. The photograph was shot during their 1975 US tour, in the New York studio.

Recently, I found an image from the same shoot in Michael Ochs's photographic archive.

... we were surrounded by all this snow. He took a load of shots outside ...
– Hugh Cornwell

While I'm on the subject, I feel I must refer to another black-and-white shot that is dear to me: *Black and White*, by the Stranglers.

The photograph is by Ruan O'Lochlainn, who has sadly died. I had a lot of difficulty finding material and information on this captivating image. What I did discover was that, despite appearances, it wasn't shot in the studio. The white you see isn't the classic neutral studio background, but snow!

Jim Sunderland, an ardent fan of the group and a family friend of Jet Black, gave me this nice insight:

Now, I can't remember whether it's something I gleaned from articles I read, or an account from friends of the group or Jet's family around 1980–81, when I used to visit their office near London Bridge. At the time, I went there almost every weekend.

What happened was this. During the winter of 1977–78, which was cold and very snowy, the Stranglers went to record their third album in a farm called Bear Shanks, in the Midlands, far from the distractions of London. It belonged to an Irish folk/pub rock musician, Ruan O'Lochlainn.

He had a recording studio but was also a photographer – or at least he had a camera. Ruan took loads of photos of the Stranglers, and one of these, retouched, became the cover photo of Black and White.

I've always had the impression that this wasn't one of those boring studio photographs...

A second important account is in an interview with Hugh Cornwell published in the *Burning Up Times*, issue number 1 – a long, detailed description of those days spent in the country. Among other things, Cornwell tells of photographs of them playing chess in the snow.

The *NME* published two photographs of the group, probably part of the same shoot, in its 28 January 1978 issue.

In 1976 Alan Betrock founded the punk magazine *New York Rocker*. It was an exceptional music publication, with a keen eye for the new music scene, new artists and new trends – it was more than simply a music periodical. I'd urge you to just open any issue, flick through it, read it and compare it with, for example, the famous *Rolling Stone*. The abyss that separates their contents will be obvious. *NYR* stood out from other magazines of the time for its content, its design – even for its advertising. There was something precious on every page. The editorial staff included a vast number of young artists and personalities who gravitated towards the punk scene: Ira Kaplan, Ken Barnes, Amos Poe and Jimmy De Sana. Often, the pictures accompanying the articles were the work of photographers at the start of their careers such as Bob Gruen, Anya Phillips and Godlis. The magazine became a sort of gallery for showing their pictures. One example is the December 1976 issue, which 'exhibited' photographs by Robert Mapplethorpe. The piece headlined 'Victor Bockris goes to the airport with Robert Mapplethorpe' included four photographs and an interesting interview.

Mapplethorpe was very close, and sensitive, to the new underground scene – he photographed Andy Warhol, Louise Bourgeois, Deborah Harry, Peter Gabriel and Grace Jones. Everyone knows the pictures he shot of Patti Smith on various occasions – especially for the cover of the album *Horses* – but far less mention is made of the cover of Television's *Marquee Moon*, perhaps because of the 'coloured mess' made by the group's guitarist, Richard Lloyd.

Apparently Mapplethorpe gave the proof prints to Television; the guitarist chose one and made come changes in colour using a photocopying machine at a printer's in Times Square. Lloyd deliberately used a process that modified colour in a completely random way. The resulting photograph was strangely coloured. It was Tom Verlaine who decided to keep it for the cover. The following extract from Victor Bockris's interview with the photographer deals with this very subject:

Victor: *You did Television's cover for their album. How's that come out?*

Robert: *I'm quite happy with the picture, I can show it to you. But they want something less professional so they're going to use a Xerox which I don't mind. I like what they're gonna do (gets portfolio to show me picture).*

Victor: *They're going to use a colour Xerox.*

Robert: *Yeah. He's a complete dictator, Tom, and it's alright because in the end he knows what he wants. You know it's not a matter of... I have the Xerox too.*

Victor: *Great. I'd love to see that.*

Robert: *That's rough (showing me colour Xerox).*

Victor: *I like the quality. I like the skin tones.*

Robert: *Nobody's used a Xerox.*

Victor: *I don't understand it. These things look really great. I love it.*

Robert: *Yeah. The thing I don't like about it is they always look the same. I mean they're always good. You can't miss. But the fact that nobody did yet... I mean that, with a really elegant black border, will look great.*

Victor: *What's their album like?*

Robert: *I don't know. I haven't heard. They're just in the studio now.*

Victor: *You shot the cover as soon as they got the contract?*

Robert: *Yeah. They wanted it immediately 'cos he was sort of fanatical about having it come out the way he wanted it so he wanted to start from the start so that he could...*

Victor: *Beginning the package first and then make the record that goes in it. That's a good idea.*

Robert: *He doesn't want the art director to touch it. I don't really like his music. It's just too abstracted for my taste.*

Victor: *But he's a very interesting guy isn't he, Tom Verlaine?*

Robert: *I guess.*

I think that *Marquee Moon* is one of the least rated covers made by a well-known photographer.

Though it lacks the essential, rough quality that marks Mapplethorpe's black-and-white images, it absolutely must have a place here, and I regret not having managed to find the alternative shots – those proofs that Lloyd bravely modified in what I'd call a totally punk act of 'artistic sharing'.

In 1978, that same environment that was fizzing with new ideas saw the release of the album *More Songs about Buildings and Food*, by the New York band Talking Heads. The cover, by the singer David Byrne, is a 'photomosaic' made up of 529 Polaroid shots of the group's four members by the artist Jimmy De Sana. A real work of art!

This cover proves how often at that time musicians, photographers, graphic designers and artists of various kinds swapped ideas and creative energy, in the process changing the shape of a movement that, superficially, might have looked like just a brief episode in youth pop music. In fact, as I have already said above, I believe it should be considered a comprehensive artistic *avant-garde* embracing a vast range of genres.

The farmer's daughter…

Here's another interesting nugget that was a 'present' from Edo Bertoglio in one of the first letters I received from him during our correspondence.

All I have left from the Parallel Lines *shoot is a group photograph. The others no longer exist; I think I gave everything to the record company they were with at the time. I had shot everything in Ektachrome (colour transparencies). I'll see whether I have anything else. But although I still have everything from that time, this shoot is missing.*

I have some photos of Madonna, which must have been for the cover of Like a Virgin, *that were paid for but never used. Do you want to see them?*

About the photographers

Roberta Bayley remains the pre-eminent photographer of the punk era. From her work at the famed CBGB club on the Bowery to her chronicle of the British punk scene, Bayley's portfolio of subjects includes Blondie, Richard Hell, the Sex Pistols, Elvis Costello, Billy Idol, Iggy Pop, Talking Heads, Television, the Clash, the Damned, the Dead Boys, the New York Dolls, Nick Lowe, Poly Styrene and X-Ray Spex and Joe Strummer. Bayley includes in her portfolio album covers for Richard Hell's *Blank Generation*, Johnny Thunder's Heartbreakers *L.A.M.F.*, and the Ramones' self-named debut album, acknowledged by *Rolling Stone* magazine as among the 100 best of the rock era.

—

After graduating in film direction and editing at the Conservatoire Libre du Cinéma Français in Paris in 1975, **Edo Bertoglio** moved first to London and later, in 1976, to New York. There he worked as a photographer for many American, Japanese, French and Italian fashion and art magazines. He regularly contributed to Andy Warhol's *Interview* from 1978 to 1982 and also worked for record companies. In 1981 he directed *Downtown 81*, a movie about a day in the life of the young artist

Jean Michel Basquiat. In 2005 he completed his second movie, *Face Addict*.

—

Born in Paris, **Alain Bizos** moved to New York in 1969 to become assistant to the artist Arman. During this time, he began working on conceptual photographic sequences. Travelling frequently between New York and France, in 1973 he participated in the creation of the daily *Libération* newspaper. A few years later, in collaboration with a group of young designers working under the name 'Bazooka', Bizos created and became Director of Publication for the monthly *Un Regard Moderne*. At the end of 1979 Bizos returned to France to act as 'artist-photographer-reporter' for the launch of *Actuel*. In 1986, he was asked to join in the creation of the 'Vu' agency.

—

During the 70s and early 80s **Willie Christie** worked extensively as a photographer with British *Vogue*, which included working closely with Grace Coddington and the late Liz Tilberis. He went on to shoot 12 *Vogue* covers and many inside spreads. His portfolio includes award-winning advertising campaigns (L'Oreal and Yves St Laurent), fashion and portrait work for

international icons (Cary Grant, Grace Jones, Douglas Fairbanks Jr, Sir John Mills, Catherine Deneuve) and rock 'n' roll album covers and portraits (Rolling Stones, Pink Floyd, David Bowie, Bryan Ferry, Lou Reed). In 1982, he began writing and directing commercials and music videos including Pink Floyd's 'Final Cut' and the first cinema commercial for 'Medway' Shoes. In 2015 Willie was in partnership with a highly regarded television production company to head up a TV show on photography.

—

Keith Collie graduated with an MA in photography from the Royal College of Art. He was appointed immediately after the course by Condé Nast to work as a photographer for *Vogue* magazine. He is affiliated to the Royal Institute of British Architects as a recognized architectural photographer. A representative of the UK at the Venice Biennale, museum collections in the UK and abroad house his work and since before the end of the last century he has been interested in the craft required for high-end digital capture and holography.

—

A native of Cork City, **Fin Costello** has photographed

many of the best-known faces in the world of rock 'n' roll over the past 40 years. Iconic pictures of Mick Jagger, Phil Lynott, Steven Tyler and Pete Townshend sit alongside intimate portraits of Rory Gallagher, Cat Stevens, Peter Gabriel and Lemmy from Motörhead. He has achieved worldwide recognition for his images of artists as diverse as Ozzy Osbourne, Cradle of Filth, Michael Jackson and Fleetwood Mac, and for album covers such as Kiss's *Alive!*, Deep Purple's *Made in Japan*, Rush's *Permanent Waves* and his award-winning cover for Japan's *Tin Drum*. His main body of work has been done for magazines like *Classic Rock*, *Rolling Stone*, *NME*, *Metal Hammer*, *Sounds* and *Music Life* in Japan, for which he has photographed AC/DC, Queen, Jeff Beck, Japan and Eric Clapton, among many others.

—

Welsh-born **Chalkie Davies** joined the rock 'n' roll circus in 1973 after photographing David Bowie's last night as Ziggy Stardust. He worked as a staff photographer at *NME* from 1975 to 1979, shooting numerous covers and features on Nick Lowe, Ian Dury, the Clash and the Ramones. In 1980 he helped launch *The Face* magazine with his old *NME* editor Nick Logan, shooting many cover stories. During this period he shot many record covers for Thin Lizzy, Elvis Costello, the Pretenders, the Specials, Pete Townshend, Robert Plant and David Bowie. He also made a series of formal portraits of many of the best musicians from that era. These unseen portraits and a selection of his best work for *NME* were exhibited in a large retrospective of his music photography at the National Museum of Wales in 2015.

—

Originally apprenticed to commercial and fashion photographers, **George DuBose** first became associated with New Wave music after he began speculative work with the fledgling B52's from Athens, Georgia. He has photographed and designed over 300 album covers, collecting 30 gold and platinum albums for groups as diverse as REM, the Go Go's, Melissa Etheridge, Kid Creole and the Coconuts, Biz Markie and Big Daddy Kane. The Ramones commissioned him to photograph or design their last nine covers and it is their only gold record, for *Ramones Mania*, that he treasures most.

As a young photographer, hanging out in the exciting New York punk/New Wave scene, DuBose was well known for his documentation of the influential New York City nightclubs, Max's Kansas City, CBGB, the Mudd Club, Hurrah, Xenon and Studio 54. Du Bose's professional experience includes staff positions as art director and photographer for Island Records and Cold Chillin' Records, the first photo editor for *SPIN* magazine and The Image Bank book division and staff photographer for the original *Interview* magazine.

—

Brian Duffy is famous above all for having immortalized the singer David Bowie on the album covers that made headlines, such as *Aladdin Sane* (1973), *Lodger* (1979) and *Scary Monsters* (1980). Along with David Bailey and Terence Donovan, Duffy is one of the 'Black Trinity', a trio that revolutionized fashion photography. From *Harper's Bazaar* to *Vogue*, the Swinging London of the sixties was immortalized by his memorable shots. Throughout the following years Duffy has collaborated with publications including *Glamour*, *Esquire*, *Town Magazine*, *Queen Magazine*, *Elle*, *The Observer*, *The Times* and the *Daily Telegraph*.

—

Born and brought up in Sussex, **Andy Earl** studied art at Trent Polytechnic in the UK. Earl was offered a show at The Photographers' Gallery in London and the following year represented Britain at the Venice Biennale. On the strength of the London show Malcolm McLaren offered him a commission for the controversial Bow Wow Wow album cover. A hugely successful career within the international music business followed, with over 120 sleeves, including 20 videos for musicians such as the Rolling Stones. (Extract from 'Icons of Pop', National Portrait Gallery)

—

Esther Friedman was born in Mannheim, Germany. In 1974 she moved to Berlin, where she worked as an apprentice for the photographer Hans Pieler. After meeting James Osterberg, aka Iggy Pop, in 1976, she followed him with her camera for seven years. In 1989, she opened an art gallery in Frankfurt. In 2013 she won the Lead Award in Gold for the Portrait Series of the Year for her photographs, published in *Zeit Magazine*, of Iggy Pop. Her work was exhibited at the Deichtorhallen in Hamburg in 2013, in a solo show at Philipp Pflug Contemporary in Frankfurt in 2015, and in Berlin in 2016. Her book *The Passenger* was published in 2013 by Knesebeck Publishers, Munich. Alongside her photography, Friedman advi- ses art collectors and corporate collections.

—

In 1968, **Chris Gabrin** studied Photography at Bournemouth Art College and then left to work for one of London's leading fashion and advertising photographers. After a few years as a freelance photographer, mainly shooting bands, he set up a studio in Camden Town, London in 1976 and subsequently photographed many acts including Elvis Costello, Ian Dury, the Stranglers, Blondie, the Damned and Motörhead. In 1980 he moved into directing and producing music videos and documentaries. He still enjoys taking photographs.

—

Peter Gravelle's photographic career spans nearly 40 years – through the early days of British punk, fashion in Italy and advertising and portraiture in America and Japan. Advertising clients include Versace Couture, Levi's and Hino Trucks, while editorial clients include *Vogue Italia*, *Harper's Bazaar* and *Vanity Fair*. Portrait commissions include Quentin Tarantino and Margaret Trudeau, among others. He has exhibited solely and in group shows in London, Berlin and Los Angeles and features as himself in Alan Parker's movie *Who Killed*

Nancy? His work is also in the permanent collections of both London's National Gallery and MoMA, New York City.

—

Brian Griffin was born in Birmingham in 1948 but lived in the Black Country until going to Manchester Polytechnic to study photography. Since 1972, he has lived in London as a freelance photographer, getting his first commission for *Management Today* in November 1972. His work was first exhibited in the Young British Photographers in 1975. In 1988 he published the book *Work* with a one-man show at the National Portrait Gallery in London. *Work* went on to be awarded the Best Photography Book in the World at the Barcelona Primavera Fotografica in 1991. In 1989 the *Guardian* newspaper proclaimed Griffin to be 'The Photographer of the Decade'. *Life* magazine used the photograph 'A Broken Frame' on its front cover of a special supplement entitled 'The Greatest Photographs Of The 80s'. On 3 March 2014 he received an Honorary Doctorate from Birmingham City University for his lifetime contribution to the City of Birmingham.

—

Martyn Goddard studied photography at Harrow College

of Art and after graduating in 1974 assisted various leading photographers before going freelance. He became part of the New Wave music scene of the 70s, working with acts such as Blondie, the Jam, Sham 69 and the Cure. In the late 1970s he was invited to contribute to the *Sunday Telegraph Magazine* where he was assigned portrait and feature shoots with some of the great personalities of the arts world, while at the same time contributing to the iconic *Car* magazine, producing automotive and travel stories. In recognition of his images, he became a Fellow of the British Institute of Professional Photography in 1987.

—

Julia Gorton's graphic black-and-white photos from the late 1970s focused on her friends, the downtown musicians who walked the streets in torn stockings, leather jackets and the cast-offs of a previous generation. Shooting with a large format Polaroid camera, then an Olympus OM-1, this work has been largely unseen except in period fanzines and on small label record jackets.

—

Bob Gruen is one of the most well-known and respected pho-

tographers in rock 'n' roll. From John Lennon to Johnny Rotten, Muddy Waters to the Rolling Stones, Elvis to Madonna, Bob Dylan to Bob Marley and Tina Turner to Debbie Harry, he has captured the music scene for over 40 years in photographs that have gained worldwide recognition.

—

Curtis Knapp lives and works in New Orleans, Louisiana. He was born in Garden City, Long Island, New York, attended the Parsons School of Design, New York, and then began a career in commercial illustration and photography in New York City. Since the 1980s he has photographed some of the greatest artists, musicians, actors, writers and celebrities of our day, including Madonna (her first portrait magazine cover), Toshiro Mifune, Steve Buscemi, William Burroughs, Jim Carroll, Lou Reed, REM, Brian Eno, Dennis Hopper, John Hurt and Andy Warhol. Knapp was based in Japan from 1984 to 2002. His work has appeared on the covers of *Time* magazine, *Playboy*, *Black + White Photography*, *Photo Technique*, and in *Le Figaro* in France and *FHM* in the UK, and has been featured in numerous magazines, including *Rolling Stone*, *Zoom*, *Vogue*, *GQ*, *Esquire*, *Le Figaro*, *FHM* and

Andy Warhol's *Interview*. Knapp has published eight books of photography, including an iTunes app book.

—

Gered Mankowitz established his first studio in Mason's Yard in 1963, in the very heart of 60s swinging London. He met and photographed Marianne Faithfull in 1964, who was managed by the mercurial Andrew Loog Oldham, who also managed the Rolling Stones. Gered started working with the Rolling Stones in 1965; he toured America with them and produced several album covers for the band. He continued working with them until 1967 by which time Gered was established as one of London's leading rock photographers. Early in 1967 Gered worked with Jimi Hendrix Experience, producing during two sessions at his Mason's Yard studio images of Jimi that would go on to become some of the most iconic and widely known portraits of the great musician.

—

After discovering the camera at the age of twelve, **Tony McGee** had by the age of seventeen worked for *Vogue* and *Harper's Bazaar*. He has photographed superstars David Bailey, Marie Helvin, Jason Statham, Daniel

Day-Lewis, Jonathan Rhys Meyers, Robbie Williams and David Bowie. His agency now works for brands such as L'Oreal, Nestlé, Nivea and Chanel.

—

From 1977 to 1981 **Eugene Merinov** trod the boards in front of the stages at CBGB, Max's Kansas City, Hurrah, Trax, Danceteria, Irving Plaza, TR3, Maxwell's, Ukrainian National Hall, Paradise Garage, The Palladium and the original Peppermint Lounge. Along the way, he became perhaps the ultimate and sharpest visual recorder of the emerging and amazing post-punk scene, with his searing shots of such greats as Bauhaus, Wire, Gang of Four, X, XTC, New Order, Monochrome Set, James Chance's Contortions, Richard Hell's Voidoids, Suicide, Pere Ubu, Lydia Lunch, Only Ones, Bush Tetras and more, all caught in their primal infancy/urgency. His shots of the band synonymous with CBGB, the Ramones, in their ancestral home, circa *Rocket to Russia*, are perhaps the best of all of them.
(Jack Rabid, Editor and Publisher, *The Big Takeover* magazine, 19 July 2007)

—

At the age of 17 **Jim Rakete** began to work professionally as a photo-journalist for newspapers, magazines and agencies. From 1977 to 1986 he ran The Factory in Berlin-Kreuzberg and was known chiefly as the music manager of Nina Hagen, Nena and Spliff. He was a decisive figure in getting German New Wave going. His pictures of Jimi Hendrix, Ray Charles, Mick Jagger, David Bowie and Herbert Grönemeyer have become icons. (Translated from German by Jonathan Uhlaner)

—

Ebet Roberts moved from her native Memphis to New York City to paint but switched to photography in 1977 when she began documenting the evolving CBGB scene. Her photographs are reproduced in innumerable publications including *Rolling Stone*, *MOJO*, *SPIN*, *GQ*, *Playboy*, *The New York Times*, *Newsweek*, *Time*, *People*, *USA Today* and *The Village Voice*. Her photographs have also been widely exhibited and are in the permanent collection of The Rock And Roll Hall of Fame, Seattle's Experience Music Project, The Grammy Museum and The Hard Rock Café.

—

Masayoshi Sukita was born in Fukuoka Prefecture in 1938. He studied under Shisui Tanahashi after graduating from the Japan Institute of Photography and Film and went on to receive APA awards in 1963 and 1968. Sukita developed an interest in subcultures after the 1969 Woodstock concert and began travelling to New York and London to shoot. Sukita met Shuji Terayama in New York in 1970 and obtained permission to take his pictures. He served as director of photography for 'Throw Away Your Books, Rally in the Street' (*Sho o suteyo machi e deyou*) in 1971. Developing an interest in T. Rex, in 1972 he travelled to Britain and succeeded in capturing unique images of the band. He met David Bowie around the same time and has been taking pictures of the artist ever since. One such portrait was used for the cover of the *Heroes* album released in 1977.

—

Rod Swenson is a multi-media conceptual artist best known for his over-the-top confrontational experiments in mass culture. Originally trained as a painter, he had a Rosenthal Scholarship to the Brooklyn Museum, and received an MFA in Painting from Yale in 1969 where he, as a self-defined 'neo-Dadaist' or 'anti-artist', was already doing conceptual and performance pieces. His work in the underground music scene included producing shows and videos for then little-known performers such as Patti Smith, the Ramones, the Dead Boys and Blondie before creating the Plasmatics, for whom he created and produced the legendary stage shows, album covers, posters and videos.

—

Seth Tillett is an artist, film maker and theatrical designer living in New York City.

An Hachette UK Company
www.hachette.co.uk

First published in Italian in 2016 by
Nomos Edizioni as *Pics Off!*
L'estetica della Nuova Onda Punk.
Fotografie e dischi 1976-1982
—

This edition published in Great Britain
in 2016 by Mitchell Beazley,
a division of Octopus Publishing Group
Ltd
Carmelite House
50 Victoria Embankment
London EC4Y 0DZ
www.octopusbooks.co.uk
www.octopusbooksusa.com

Copyright © Nomos Edizioni 2016
English translation copyright ©
Octopus Publishing Group 2016
—

Distributed in the US by Hachette
Book Group
1290 Avenue of the Americas
4th and 5th Floors
New York, NY 10020
—

Distributed in Canada by Canadian
Manda Group
664 Annette St.
Toronto, Ontario, Canada M6S 2C8

ISBN 978-1-78472-149-7

A CIP catalogue record for this book is
available from the British Library.

Printed and bound in Italy

10 9 8 7 6 5 4 3 2 1

Credits

Publisher's credits
for the English edition
Commissioning Editor
Joe Cottington
Creative Director
Jonathan Christie
Design
Jeremy Tilston
Editorial Assistant
Ella Parsons
Translation
Simon Jones
Senior Production Manager
Katherine Hockley

Publisher's credits for the Italian
edition
Project Director
Matteo Torcinovich
Art direction and design
Sebastiano Girardi, Matteo Rosso
Layout
Elena Antonutti
Text
Matteo Torcinovich, Glenn O'Brien,
George DuBose, Alberto Lot
Editing and translation from English
Anna Albano
Photo Consultant
Catia Zucchetti, Marina Itolli

Photo Credits

Front cover © Martyn Goddard
p. 21 © Bob Gruen / www.bobgruen.com
pp. 23, 24, 25, 27 © Roberta Bayley/
Getty Images
pp. 29, 30, 31, 77 © Edo Bertoglio
pp. 33, 34, 35, 36, 37 © Martyn
Goddard
pp. 39, 40, 41 © Esther Friedman
pp. 43, 44, 45 © William Christie
pp. 47, 48, 49, 63, 64, 65 © George-
DuBose.com
pp. 51, 52, 53 © Seth Tillett
pp. 55, 56, 57, 59, 60, 61 © Julia
Gorton
p. 67 © Brian Griffin
pp. 70, 71, 72 © Curtis Knapp
pp. 73, 74, 75 © Rod Swenson
Licensed through Pandemonium
Merchandising LLC
pp. 79, 80, 81, 82, 83 © 1980 Ebet
Roberts
pp. 85, 86, 87 © Esther Friedman
pp. 91, 92, 93, 95, 96 © Peter Gravelle
pp. 97, 113, 185 © Chris Gabrin
pp. 99, 100, 101, 102, 103, 139, 140,
141 © Martyn Goddard
pp. 105, 106, 107, 123, 124, 125,
126, 127, 128, 129, 135, 136, 137 ©
Gered Mankowitz BOWSTIR Ltd.20015/
Mankowitz.com
pp. 109, 110, 111 (© 1977 / 1997
Risky Folio, Inc. Courtesy of The David
Bowie Archive ™), 143, 144, 145, 147
© Photo by Masayoshi Sukita
pp. 115, 116, 117, 118, 119 © Keith
Collie
pp. 120, 121, 149, 150, 151, 167,
168, 169, 181, 182, 183, 187, 195,
196, 197 © Brian Griffin
pp. 131, 132, 133 © Jim Rakete
pp. 153, 154, 155 © Tony McGee
pp. 157, 158, 159, 160, 161 © Alain
Bizos
pp. 163, 164, 165, 177, 178, 179 ©
Chalkie Davies
pp. 171, 172, 173, 174, 175 Photo
Duffy©Duffy Archive
p.189 © Andy Earl
pp. 191, 192, 193 © Fin Costello
pp. 199, 200, 201, 202, 203 © Eugene
Merinov.